POWERED

BY WELLESLEY

Jin Lan McCann

©2017 JIN LAN MCCANN

ALL RIGHTS RESERVED

ISBN-13: 978-0-9989899-4-5

AUTHORED BY JIN LAN MCCANN

EDITED BY NEWGRANGE PRESS

COVER DESIGNED BY: ALEXANDER VALCHEV

This book is dedicated to all kind hearted progressive people and all the young people in the world.

FOREWORD

Dear readers,

To tell the truth, or not to tell the truth?
That is the question.

We can never afford not to. So, this book will reveal some very uncomfortable truths that may alienate some people whom I whole heartedly love and respect. I hope my journey and insights may inspire you to revisit the historical events mentioned in this book and your biases, with an open mind.

Yes, with an open mind. Is it easy? I thought I was an open minded modern Chinese woman when I came to the US in 2001. The truth is that my mind had been closed like the shell of an oyster until 2018. Why 2018? Why not in 2001, the year I first stepped onto US soil, the supposed land of the free? Why not in 2009, the year I entered Wellesley College, one of the most prestigious schools in the US? Because, in none of these years were my instilled communist beliefs changed but enhanced.

Donald J. Trump's victory in the presidential election in 2016 had totally disrupted my belief system. I could not believe that my alma mater's beloved alumna Hillary R. Clinton could lose the election, especially with a majority of the popular vote. Many alumnae cried when the result was announced. I did too.

So, I spent two years extensively researching what happened to my beliefs. Among my transformation was an astonishing epiphany: that God indeed exists, though I was born an atheist. The understanding of God/Nature not only helped me to understand the conservative wisdom, but also the history of rising China and its impacts upon the world. Such a transformation is not easy for someone like me, who had, for most of my lifetime, been brainwashed by the atheist communist party.

So, I decided to rewrite my memoir in brutally honest fashion, to provide you a small, yet unclouded, window into China's soul, through my personal evolution and insights.

In this book, I will try to demonstrate:
1) How Reaganomics/Trickledown Economics guided China's economic reform and lifted 1.3 billion people out of extrem poverty, as viewed through my personal life experiences;
2) How lacking the guidance of Reaganomics/Trickledown Economics brought down the American Empire in the world competition;
3) My urge to awaken the American people and revalue the devalued conservative/ancient wisdom.

My dear readers, please fasten your seatbelt. The adventure ahead will be stormy and thrilling. Enjoy!

Oct 25, 2019

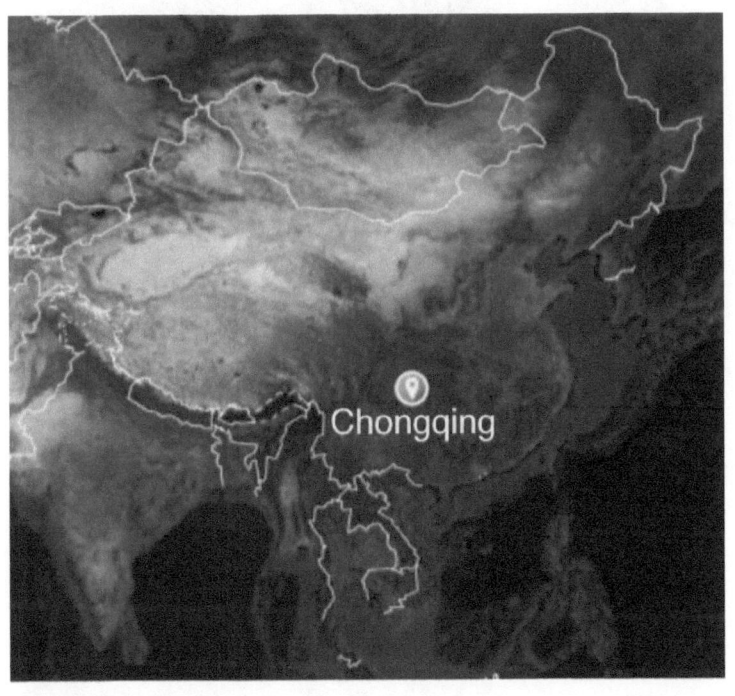

Map of the People's Republic of China

Pictures of Chongqing

Pictures of Chongqing

Contents

I. Foreword
II. Wellesley Women are Growing Roots and Wings
III. Rising China
- Splendid Morning Dew..1
- My Mother...42
- My Father..53
- Cruising On The Yangtze...59
- Development On Dry Land..77
- Love In A Prison..84
- Dancing With Wolves..89
- Diving Into The Sea of Commerce................................98
- Boyfriend Transplant..123
- My Next Port Of Call: A Pirate Smuggler.....................130
- The Pirate In Chains...137
- Two Bullets Fly By...143
- My Godot Appears..156
- A Blue Eyed Bear...175
- The Bear Caves..185
- Could The 2008 Debacle Have Been Avoided?....204
- Cutting The Deck...211
- Empowered By Wellesley...219

IV. The Falling American Empire..246
V. Afterword...260

WELLESLEY WOMEN ARE GROWING ROOTS AND WINGS

On the beautiful campus of Wellesley College, a blue banner with white letters says, "Wellesley Women Are Growing Roots and Wings." On my coffee mug I read the words, "Wellesley College - Where the Coffee is Strong, the Women Stronger." Yes, this school empowers women to change the world for the better.

I entered Wellesley College in 2009 to prepare myself to grow in the "Free World". Since Chairman Mao died in 1976, my life had been improving each year with the rapid growth of China. However, that trend stoped once I graduated from Wellesley College. I was told that I couldn't grow because I didn't have a college degree. This excuse came out to be false. I was told that there no growth of the working class because the US was already fully developed. I believed this shallow or dishonest explanation for over a decade.

In what is called 'middle age', I found myself at a prestigious women's school gathered together with the smartest people in the world seeking truths; a dream which I could never conjure began to unfold.

On campus, I was always presented with the question: "What brought you to Wellesley?" The question invariably transports me to my hometown Chongqing, and childhood.

Chongqing is the largest and most populous city in China, although people in the West might not even know it exists. It's a mountain city, a gateway to Southwestern

China, and the economic center of the upper Yangtze River. It has 32 million residents, a number increasing by 500,000 per year, two digital annual growth. It is the 3rd largest center of automobile manufacturing, and the largest motorcycle-manufacturing region in the country. More than one hundred Fortune 500 companies have established a presence in the city. This rising metropolis is reported as having beautiful and courageous women, because people can see their vibrance all over the world, especially, in the cities where the living rhythms are fast. They are not afraid to show the world their beauty, and they are not afraid to leave their comfort zones. They are the nut crackers.

As this preface is composed, the American people have rejected a Wellesley graduate who has the reputation of spending her life fighting for women's rights as its first woman President. Many of us shed tears over this unbelievable defeat. Our tears did not help our understanding of what went wrong.

However, if the United States is strong enough to adopt and nurture a willowy Chinese woman and turn her into a force for change, it can survive anything. We shall see, shall we not? As the reader is led along the twisted and rocky path of the fantastic story of my life, a tale illuminated through the lens of post-Cultural Revolution history, he or she will conclude that the audacity of hope trumps any lesser emotion.

SPLENDID MORNING DEW

MY PLACE OF BIRTH

I just translated my talented high school classmate's new poem from Chinese into English:

Birth Place

Whenever I needed to fill in a birth place form,
I always sincerely inscribed:
'Chongqing Obstetrics and Gynecology Hospital'.
Every time, someone pointed out:
You only need to write down 'Chongqing,'
Every time, I stubbornly shook my head.

I knew, during those disastrous years,
to safeguard the same idol,
even family members would kill each other.
This city owned numerous weaponry manufactures,
working class members drove tanks into the streets,
set sail warships upon the Yangtze River,
targeted schools with canons . . .
For one born in a Hospital,
life was guaranteed from the beginning.

How lucky this was,
but more people in my time

*were given birth on narrow, humid
hard boards in the darkness,
in the range of flying bullets,
in the domain of missile explosion coverage.
Their first cry could not break through
the cotton quilt insulated windows,
even some of them died before their first cry
could be delivered to earth.
     - By Yu Yan, 2016[1]*

Yu Yan and I are high school classmates, we were both born in Chongqing in February 1967, the beginning of the notorious Cultural Revolution, China's 'dark age'. This poem is a depiction of the crazy environment into which we were born. However, my other friends who were teenagers at that time, told me what they *saw* was much worse than the poem *depicted*.

My Mom used to recall the armed fighting during the beginning of the Cultural Revolution. She thought that it was supposed to be a civilized debate about how people should run the country. Instead, the losers of the forensic debate resorted to violent repression of each other, because Chairman Mao Ze Dong[2] said "Power comes from guns." The people

---

[1] This poem is very current. Why does it appear now? Because, if history doesn't necessarily repeat, at least it rhymes. Both Yu Yan and I observed that China is on the cust of repeating history. Whether this society can avoid repetition of past tragedies is many people's concern.

[2] Please know that Chairman Mao Ze Dong will hereinafter be referred to as Mao. High officials and celebrities will be given their original full names in Chinese order, which is the last name first,

treated what he said to be Gospel, with the same reverence Westerners accord the words of the Bible.

Mom used to complain to me that sometimes she did not even have food to eat for a whole day, while hiding in the bomb shelter to avoid flying bullets and eyeless missiles. However, I, an infant, kept crying in her arms for milk. Now I feel sorry for her and wish I could have been a better infant.

GRANDPA PISSES HIMSELF

The name of my eldest brother is History, given by my Mom's father, Clean Life[3]. History is seven years my senior. He told me a story about the bomb shelter era.

One day, when all my family members were hiding in the bomb shelter under the building of the Yangtze Shipping Co., where my Father worked, my Grandfather became so hungry he had to make some food to eat. Thus, he desperately fled home with my brother History. Since my Grandfather did not want to see the flying bullets outside the uncurtained window, he draped the window with a bed sheet. While he was standing on a stool so doing, a bullet broke through the glass window and lodged in the wall. In shock, he fell to the ground, cried out, and sprayed himself with

---

followed by the first name. For teachers and clients, I will only give their last names without translation.

[3] Clean Life is my maternal Grandfather's name. Chinese people's names usually represent parents' expectations of their children. However, read through my stories: you will find that, sometimes, the character of particular individual developes contrary to the meaning of his or her name.

urine. History thought this most funny and laughed at my Grandfather.

My brother told this story to me when he was 37. I told him it was *not* funny because my Grandfather could have been killed by that bullet. How lucky for History that he was too young to realize fear.

THE PARABLE OF THE STEAM BUN

Besides the concepts of class struggle and anti-American Empiralism, hunger was the most enduring image of my childhood. In 1970, at the age of three, I remember one morning when my Mom slept very late, my Father had gone to work, and my two elder brothers were at school. I ate a steam bun that my Father bought for me, gobbled it down fast. Not satisfied, I cruised around the table that held one lonesome steam bun. *That* one belonged to my Mom. I circled the table again and again, never taking my eyes off the bun.

I thought: 'the extra parts of the bun shaped by the steam container's bottom slats, should not *really* belong to the bun.' So, I tore those segments off and devoured them. Still not satisfied, I walked around my Mom's bed, and spoke to the air again and again: "One bun is so small, not enough."

Then, I walked back to the table and gazed at my Mom's steam bun and thought: "If the bun doesn't have the *skin*, it still can be called a bun." I tore the skin off and ate it. Still, not satisfied, I walked back to my Mom's bed, said to her: "You have such a big bun, I do not know how you can eat it all." Mom was surprised, but she did not say a word.

Years later, she questioned me: "How can a bun be too small for a small person and too big for a big person?"

Then, our neighbor, Uncle Song, the police chief, opened the door and asked me why my Mom did not get up and cook. He did not see our stove blazing in our common kitchen. I told him that my Mom was still sleeping. He came in and put his hand on my Mom's head, then suddenly picked her up and carried her away.

I became impatient, waiting until my second brother Banyan came home from school. He was four years older than me. He was the naughty sibling who caused trouble every day and enjoyed beating me whenever we encountered each other. Banyan came in and immediately grabbed the bun on the table and devoured it.
I yelled at him: "That's Mom's bun!"
He answered: "Mom won't be home soon, because she is sick and must have an operation at the hospital."

I remember this vividly, because I never desired steam buns as much as in that year. Also, later in that year, we acquired an additional room on the third floor instead of sharing one studio without a kitchen nor a toilet. We obtained this extra room, because my grandfather had contracted T.B.

We were a family of six. My Grandfather, parents, two elder brothers and myself shared that studio since my parents' marriage. Such was the norm at that time in our society, and we were not the worst off, because my Father was the party secretary of a branch of the Yangtze Shipping Company, the largest company in town. So, he could afford to let my Mom be a house wife.

In order to understand my childhood, one must understand what the Cultural Revolution is, how it happened, what its impacts are and why it is controversial.

WHAT IS THE CULTURAL REVOLUTION?

Some Westerners misunderstand the Cultural Revolution as a period during which the Chinese bureaucracy repressed its people. This can only be true if you call Orwellian repression 'government', since everyone was spying on everyone else during that time. My parents told me that bureaucratic machine was disabled by the Red Guards, who were teenage students encouraged by party Chairman Mao, and they began to play at governance. So, the Cultural Revolution is one good example of how a left-wing pure communist society becomes anarchic.

It was a violent movement initiated by Mao, in the name of democracy, to restore ideologically pure communism (Maoism)[4] – as distinguished from the pragmatic socialism implemented by state Chairman Liu Shao Qi. Liu was Mao's internal political rival in the communist party. Mao, obviously, did not want to be China's George Washington, a man who left power after two terms as the first president of the United States.

The full name of the movement is **The Great Proletarian Cultural Revolution.** It also marked Mao's return of

---

[4] If you view communism as charging 100% income taxes, laissez-faire capitalism as charging 0% income taxes, then anything between is a different level of socialism. Mao's Great Leap Forward is an example of 100% income taxes, because, even a private chicken was not allowed then.

power from his failed experiment in pure communism, the Great Leap Forward, with disastrous outcomes including genocidal famine. Maoism functioned like monotheism during the dark age of Europe. It was the only belief permissible if one wanted to survive.

In retrospect, the elements of the Cultural Revolution are: mind control, destruction of the rule of law and traditional wisdom, demonizing the West, disrespect for intellectuals, and violation of basic human rights. These elements were not only factors in forming the constructs of my early childhood, they are still a kind of active today in governing the daily lives of Chinese people, but better than before.

HOW AND WHY DID THE CULTURAL REVOLUTION BEGIN?

When the Chinese Communist Party seized power from the Qiang Kai Shek government[5] in 1949, Mao became both the chairman of the communist party *and* the state with two five-year terms. In order to turn China into a modern industrialized country at breakneck speed, Mao abandoned the communist party's promise of developing democracy, yet allowing a portion of the economy to be private.

In 1958, he started a Great Leap Forward movement that prohibited private businesses, even home kitchens. This movement caused the deaths of about 36 million human beings from starvation. In Xin Yang, Henan Province, folks feasted on the dead bodies of their neighbors. A teenage girl

---

[5] Qiang Kai Shek's government escaped to Tai Wan towards the end of the Civil War in 1949.

killed her four-year-old brother and consumed his body, and a dying mother apologized to her daughter that she only left her heart for the daughter to consume, according to Yang Ji Sheng[6], a former journalist from China's state news agency-Xin Hua.

The manpower that should have been used on food production was misallocated to produce steel and weapons. This concentration was fueled by paranoia and Xenophobia, because Mao believed that war was the norm of the world since he had never seen peace in his life. Ironically, one could see slogans like, "Be prepared against war, be prepared against natural disasters, and do everything for the people", everywhere. Then, food was stored in barns and people allowed to die.

Mao made people believe that the escaped Qiang Kai Shek government might retaliate against mainland China someday, or, foreign empires, such as the US and the USSR, might again invade China. Almost all levels of government exaggerated local outputs of food while, in fact, there was little stored in granaries.

Due to Mao's failed practice of pure communism during his two terms in office (1949-1959), the succeeding Chairman of the State, Liu Shao Qi, adopted a pragmatic strategy. He redistributed land and other resources to families. His polices improved the economy significantly in a couple of years. However, his economic success came with the price of social conflicts.

Chinese history customarily awards participants in revolution government office upon victory, no matter their level

---

[6] https://en.wikipedia.org/wiki/Yang_Jisheng_(journalist)

of competence. There was a significant number of uneducated peasant leaders in the government after Mao's accession to power in 1949. The cadre of educated leaders wanted their uneducated colleagues gone.

Since the redistribution of resources were not uniformly fair, an enormous group of uneducated people complained. They believed that the new policies meant a switch towards a capitalist, instead of a communist economy as the party promised. They complained about the arrogance of educated elites which had torn down peasant houses to build airports or other public facilities without proper negotiation with the property users. They also complained about other corruptions, such as unfair distribution of job opportunities among the politically connected, in derogation of unconnected families. Mao received massive complaints against the bureaucracy, and heard that the peasants were kneeling in front of the cadres begging for justice.

Mao seized this opportunity to attack the new administration. He pointed out that the peasants were supposed to be the owners of the country and should stand up to the authorities. Instead, they were kneeling before the authorities begging for justice. Thus, **the seeds of the Cultural Revolution were sewn**.

In May 1966, Mao accused the Liu Shao Qi government of infiltrating the society with bourgeois elements. He started the Cultural Revolution to remove capitalist roots by a continuous class struggle, breaking traditions and challenging authorities. He initiated the revolution in Qing Hua University's high school by sending his wife Jiang Qing to relay his wishes.

In response, youth groups around the country formed Red Guard units responding to Mao's appeal. They behaved as fanatically loyal Maoists. They still so behave today.

The government brainwashed the society with pure communist ideology, daily, for a decade, under Mao's rule (1949-1959). To protect the party's legitimate image, Chairman Liu Shao Qi did not openly criticize Mao's wrong economic policies, although they killed millions of people. The movement by the brainwashed Red Guards swiftly spread all over the country infiltrating the military, urban workers, and the Communist Party infrastructure itself. Teenagers left their schools and jumped on trains to go to Beijing to parade before Mao, with Mao's Red Book in everyone's hand.

Revolutionary slogans appeared everywhere on the sides of vehicles and walls of buildings. Slogans like "Long Live the Invincible Thoughts of Mao Ze Dong!" and "Long live the Proletariat Cultural Revolution!" blossomed everywhere. Many contained obvious fallacies and perverted common sense, such as "Long Live the Proletariat Dictatorship." This slogan sounds as though the people would be happy to remain poor forever. Another slogan proclaimed, "We would rather have socialist grass instead of capitalist sprouts." This sounds like "We would rather eat grass than real human food."

To get rid of the 'capitalist sprouts', the Red Guards purged all leaders who supported Chairman Liu Shao Qi and vice Chairman Deng Xiao Ping. Since Liu Shao Qi failed to communicate with the student leaders and resorted to suppression of their most radical elements, he was tortured to death by the Red Guards. Mao had to incarcerate Vice Chairman Deng Xiao Ping to protect him from being killed by

Mao's fanatic followers. Premier Zhou En Lai was once locked up in his own office by the Red Guards.

    The Cultural Revolution was conducted in the name of democracy and characterized as a civilized political campaign. However, millions of people were violently repressed and abused across the country once the zealous Red Guards tasted majority power. Basic human rights were violated. Public humiliation, arbitrary imprisonment, torture, sustained harassment, and seizure of private property were not uncommon during the time. Tian Han,[7] who wrote the revolutionary national anthem, was condemned as an anti-revolutionary revisionist and died in jail. Many people, mostly scholars and urban highschool graduates, were unwillingly displaced from their hometowns to rural regions. Historical relics and artworks were destroyed, cultural and religious sites ransacked, old and foreign books were confiscated or burned, and family ethics were abandoned. It was into this chaos that I was born.

---

[7] He is shown in picture 4.

Picture 1. Expel the traitor, hidden traitor, scab Liu Shao Qi from the party forever

Picture 2. Thoroughly expose and criticize Liu Shao Qi's monstrous crime of treason

Picture 3. This cartoon denounces Liu Shao Qi's pro-free market

Picture 4. Anti-revolutionary revisionist Tian Han

WHAT ARE THE IMPACTS OF THE CULTURAL REVOLUTION?

Normally, societies must achieve balance between competition and cooperation to develop efficiently. Competition may improve our individual strength while encouraging greed. Cooperation may integrate individual strengths while testing our tolerance and persistence. To achieve fair competition and cooperation, societies must establish and maintain the rule of law while abandoning archaic traditions, inevitably the byproducts of 'success'. However, while the Cultural Revolution accomplished the goals of shattering traditions and challenging authority, it destroyed the nascent foundation of the 'rule of law' in China, and the ability of its people to think rationally.

I discern only one positive impact of the Cultural Revolution. That is, it boosted the confidence of the poor people to be owners of the country as they broke tradition and challenged authorities. The Cultural Revolution made poor people feel proud for the first time in Chinese history, because they thought that a communist China meant that they were no longer chattels of the powerful, but owners of the country.

However, I can also discern at least three negative impacts of the Cultural Revolution. When the Red Guards shut down government and churches, then raided households, they destroyed the tenuous foundation of the rule of law and traditional civility within the society. Since then, Chinese people have developed the habit of ignoring or circumventing rules. If you see a pedestrian walking in the street of New

York City against a red light, that pedestrian may well be from mainland China. Try driving there.

In addition, the society's rational thinking deteriorated by slavish adherence to a political correctness demanded by Maoists. With freedom of thought monopolized by Maoism, it became the only philosophy acceptable to the devoted Red Guards. One had to take risks to tell the truth. The mythology of Maoism was a species of fake news.

To prove their loyalty to Mao, family members started to spy on each other, and report imagined political incorrectness. Many of the reported family members were sent to the countryside for indoctrination. Family loyalty was severely shattered.

WHY IS THE CULTURAL REVOLUTION CONTROVERSIAL?

It is controversial because Chairman Mao made us believe that the Cultural Revolution was a great revolution and should be continued forever because class struggle was eternal and inevitable[8]. This is contrary to what the post-Mao government told us. After getting rid of the Gang of Four[9] and Mao's appointed successor Chairman Hua Guo Feng, the post-Mao government characterized the Cultural Revolution as a terrible mistake made by Mao. As stated in People's Daily - repeatedly - the Cultural Revolution caused ten

---

[8] Mao said: "Class Struggle has to be discussed daily, monthly and yearly." We had to recite this quote daily when I was young.
[9] Gang of Four, led by Mao's wife Jiang Qing, tried to purify the new regime with Mao's radical left-wing ideaology, but was defeated by the right-wing power led by Deng Xiao Ping.

years of social chaos and wasted a generation's optimum time for education and economic development.

The government has never revealed to us what led Mao to make this mistake in his last ten years of life[10], and why there was such massive support for his terrible error. The government just proclaimed: "Let's not play at class struggle any more, and revalue the devalued ancient wisdom of Chinese civilization and western civilization; development is the only top priority and our ancient ancestors were good at that." The famous quote of Deng Xiao Ping, "No matter it's a white cat or black cat, as long as it can catch mice, it must be a good cat," was uttered at this time. Its purpose was to encourage people to abanond the debate on whether China should continue along the communist route or turn to the capitalist route.

So, the topic of the Great Famine caused by Mao's Great Leap Forward is still a taboo today. Rumors abounded then and now: some people believe Mao loved power too much and used innocent people's trust to attack his political rivals; others believe that it was a power struggle between the educated and uneducated leaders. Yet others believe there was a political struggle between the radical communists and the right-wing leaning communists. The truth could comprise all these elements.

---

[10] One must remember, at the inception of the Cultural Revolution, Mao was 74 years of age. He was absolutely married to his own paradigms. Marriage to paradigms at that age guarantees intellectual decay. Its analogous, in a way, to why a 1950 Hudson Hornet today is worth 20 or 30 times the price it sold for then. Some septuagenarian, married to his paradigms, is behind the wheel. From an intellectual point of view, Mao did not age gracefully. Nor did he continue to write love poems.

Goaded by Mao, the Red Guards pursued eradication of capitalist roots, because communist doctrine stipulated that capitalism may only help the 'haves' to exploit the 'have nots.' The Red Guards viewed all small private businesses, or land distribution to families, even home raised chickens and pigs, as seeds of capitalism. This is certainly true, but their belief in capitalism as a sin is wrong.

A Sino-strain of Marxism has been taught in schools. We were taught that monopolies were bad, because the monopolists let the rich intentionally waste food while allowing the poor to go hungry, despite the government monopolized everything and everyone. The anti-Hooverism arguments *post* depression in the United States mirrored these philosophies. Lectures given us emphasized competition was bad. Competition, we were told, forced the failure of many businesses and caused their owners to jump from buildings.

No one dared point out that the essence of capitalism is fair competition: *fair at the starting point - with no entry barriers*. Capitalism complies with the rules of nature, including greed. Moderately but firmly regulated with Anti-Trust law, it may eliminate the exploitation of surplus from both workers and consumers.

Mao never admitted or realized that the constant high unemployment rates and shortages of almost everything were the results of nationalizing the country's all resources. Instead, he blamed the Soviet Union for our shortage of everything, since it required repayment of loans. Or, he blamed our shortage of food on the weather.

GROWING UP IN ONE ROOM

I have never understood why my parents isolated me in one room in my early years, without sufficient communication or interaction. After the age of three and until his death, I encountered my Grandfather and my two elder brothers only at lunch and dinnertime.

Usually, as a family, we had no communication at all. Mom told us not to talk while eating. After each meal, it was time for me to go back to their bedroom which was on the third floor. The isolation lasted until bedtime when my parents returned, and was broken by meal times when my Mom brought me down to the room which my Grandfather and two elder brothers shared.

I was usually alone in the room on the third floor.

My entertainment consisted of watching the Yangtze River roll along beneath the window, or listening to the external loudspeakers repeatedly broadcasting quotes from Chairman Mao's red books, songs in praise of him or of the Cultural Revolution, all day long, each and everyday.

Naturally, I remember Mao's quotes much more than my parents' remarks since my parents barely spoke. Once, when I got bored because I had no toys at all and no one to talk to, I saw a corner of my Mom's silk shirt sticking out from a locked leather suitcase. I pulled more fabric out of the case and found that it had pandas on it, so I embroidered all of them with thick blue cotton thread.

When my Mom decided to wear that shirt, and found out what I had done to it, I got beaten with her tailor-made bamboo switch. My parents had the reputation of beating their children the hardest of any parents in our community. Their standards did not allow us to make any mistakes.

My Mom insisitd on cleaning every corner of each room every day, and always made sure I was just as clean. She accomplished this by giving me a bath and washing my hair. Each time this ritual made me feel as if I were boiling in hell. She always made sure that the water was hot enough for her, but too hot for me.

I was only a baby.

I still remember beating her face with my little fists while she was washing my hair. Of course, I also cried and screamed: "Beat you the son of tortoise! Beat you the son of tortoise!" (this is the equivalent of a well-known English curse)

My Mom scrubbed me all over until I was thirteen. Only later, I calculated it took her two hours to wash me, each time. As I grew older, I used to joke with her after she finished washing me, "Only then was I ready to serve." She believed she did so out of love, even though she was boiling me. I did feel her deep love though, because she spent so much time and energy on making sure I was always clean. Being clean was always a priority above all other things in my Mom's view.

Although I do not have any interesting memories other than painful ones about my childhood, I always believed that my Mom did everything for my benefit. Though I have never resented her, I always wanted to get away from her[11]. I barely got a chance to leave the room. Whenever I was permitted to play outside for a while, I wanted to stay as far from her regime as I could get.

I remember one night when I was four or five, I was permitted to play outside of the room with neighbor kids all night long because the heat incinerated the room and we had no electric fan. I felt so happy that night, and did not want to return home at all, even though I knew my Mom was looking for me throughout the building. At midnight, I was hiding in the dark of the corridor while watching my Mom desperately searching and calling, "Third sister, third sister. . ." I did not answer her even when she was very close to me, until I became so sleepy and I could not keep my eye lids from closing. Only then, did I respond to her.

PRIMARY SCHOOL EDUCATION

People might wonder whether I had a real name, since my Mom called me 'Third sister'. I did not hear the name 'Jin Lan' until I was six and a half, in the fall of 1973 during my first day of elementary school.

That morning, Mom pulled out a piece of paper, wrote three beautiful words on it, "Deng, Jin Lan," and taught me how to read it. She told me that this was my name. Deng is my family name from my Father, Jin means Splendid and Lan means Morning Dew. She explained to me that she and my Father had always wanted a daughter after

---

[11] This mentality is similar to how Chinese people trust the party/government although there is limited freedom of expression. I also learned, from a Yugoslovakian immigrant, that it was the same in his country.

having two sons. So, when I arrived as the answer to their dreams, they did not let my Grandfather, the most educated man in the family, name me as he did my two older brothers.

Mom loved the word 'Jin' because it was derived from a Chinese idiom, "Jin Shang Tian Hua," inscribed on each of their rice bowls received as wedding gifts. This idiom means "Adding a flower to an already splendid life." 'Lan' was my Father's idea, because Mom was The Flower in his eyes, so I was the morning dew on his flower.

I loved my name Splendid Morning Dew. However, it was too hard to write in Chinese, and until then, no one had ever taught me to read or write. Mom told me to remember my name and when the teacher called it out, I should answer.

Another thing I have never understood is why my Mom did not take me to school on the first day. She let me follow the neighbor's kid to a school where I had never been. Didn't she know that I barely left our building before, and did not have a clue where the roads led? Or how a school day works? When she told me to follow the other kids to school, I did not imagine what might happen, just ran like a *wild horse,* a name used by my Father refer to me instead of 'Jin Lan'. I didn't complain. Perhaps, I wanted to escape from Mom no matter what.

Since I had never attended a kindergarten like the rest of the kids whose parents were both working, I thought that there was only one class in each school day. In fact, there were five, three in the morning and two in the afternoon. The first class was Chinese, taught by a very beautiful woman, teacher Gong, who spoke elegant mandarin and had beautiful hand writing. I loved every second of her lecture.

After the first class, I did not know there were more classes and walked to the gate of the school. Another student saw me and told me I was going the wrong way. So, I followed her to another room on the second floor.

It was a music classroom with a harmonica in the left corner beside the blackboard. The music teacher taught us a song about Sino-American friendship, I still remember one phrase: "I love Beijing-Washington, Children of China and America laugh out loud, song of friendship throughout the world . . ." This confused me, because in movies I had seen people usually shout slogans such as, "Down with American Imperialism!" I mentally archived this confusion and enjoyed this class, but still did not know there was yet another class after this as well.

When the second class was over, I left the music classroom and walked out of the school gate. Once out of the school, I walked all the way to a crossroad, at which point I did not know which way I should go to get home. Looking at the sky and the overhead wires for trolley buses hanging down, I recalled one girl asking another whether she knew how to get home. The girl said, "Yes, my mom told me that I would never go wrong if I follow the overhead wires, because one way leads to her office, and the other way to home."

Since I knew her mom worked for the same company where my Father worked, and my home was on the opposite of my Father's office - aha!

I would just follow the overhead wires, too. I trailed a trolley bus for about ten minutes, along a street with interesting shops, and came to another cross road. There was nothing which looked familiar, so I turned around and followed another trolley bus which led me to my home.

I was so excited after my first day of school, I did not know I had missed a mathematics class. When my neighbor came home, she told me I was noted as absent from my mathematics class. I felt so embarrassed, but my Mom did not notice this.

I asked her why the American Empire that we were trying to beat down suddenly had become our friend. Mom took a piece of an old newspaper that had a picture of Dr. Henry Kissinger[12] shaking hands with Chairman Mao on it and said, "Since Dr. Kissinger visited Chairman Mao, we are no longer enemies." She said it was good for China to have America as our friend instead of as our enemy, but she did not say why.

I maintained this confusion for more than 30 years, until one day when I told a high school classmate that I saw Dr. Kissinger performing in a magic show on the stage of the Bohemian Grove in California. My classmate said he always liked Dr. Kissinger. We grew up knowing his name and he changed our lives for the better. Later, I realized that Dr. Kissinger's visit to China not only meant more freedom and prosperity for China, but also meant improvement of world peace. He ended the cold war and tactfully set China, this giant boat, on a correct course toward an advanced civilization.

But back to medieval Chongqing: the same afternoon, I went back to school and a senior student read us a story of Chairman Mao. Then we were told that we would have a big conference criticizing 'Lin' and 'Kong' the next day. Lin had

---

[12] I never dreamed that, someday, I would meet this American hero, who turned out to be one of my husband's treasured friends.

SPLENDID MORNING DEW 23

Pictures of Chairman Mao Meeting Dr. Kissinger and President Nixon

been the vice Chairman of the country before his airplane crashed two years before. Kong, pinyin for Confucius, had been dead for almost 2, 500 years. I was told we had to prepare for this critique and each one of us would be required to get on the stage and speak out.

Of course, I could not write a speech since I only knew three words, "Mao Zhu Xi" which means Chairman Mao, because it was inscribed everywhere. I still could not write my own name! The next day, I brought with me a speech my eldest brother History wrote out for me.

When my turn came, I bravely stepped onto the stage, pretended that I could read as well as my senior student who read us a Mao's story. Of course, I could only pretend for less than one minute. My teacher took away my paper and read the part criticizing Lin, who allegedly betrayed Mao, and then, criticizing Confucius, the great thinker, educator and philosopher that Chinese people had worshiped for over 2500 years.

Basically, the speech repeated what Mao said: "We should challenge the authorities, because it was their dogma which retarded the development of our Chinese people. Confucianism emphasized obedience and warned against challenging authority, because he only spoke for the ruling class, not the working class." I only realized thirty years later that this was not true.

The Cultural Revolution persisted for ten years. Mao allowed the Red Guards to torture to death his longtime revolutionary fellow fighter and comrade, Chairman Liu Shao Qi. Instead of letting the government listen to their voices, the Red Guards shut them up and sent many of the educated elites (and whoever else disagreed with them) to live with pigs and cows, in the countryside[13].

Class Struggle games transpired every day and everywhere for a decade. Mao instructed his people to never stop. Now I believe that if Dr. Kissinger did not sneak into China and talk to Mao in 1971, God himself only knows whether the great famine might have occurred again, since there was no *internal force* powerful and skillful enough to influence a change in China's political direction.

So, though my education started late, but began at a pretty high level. That a six-year old kid was required to criticize an almost 2,500-year old philosopher was a big joke to my Grandfather who was very well educated. When my naughty brother Banyan remarked that my Grandfather looked like a bad guy because he had a beard like Confucius from the cartoons, my Grandfather[14] responded that it would be *great* if he could be Confucius! Banyan and I both thought my Grandfather was anti-revolutionary, a state of mind considered extremely dangerous at that time. He could have been put in jail if he had said the same thing to someone outside of the family.

After I had learned how to count, I realized that the slogan "Chairman Mao Lives for Ten Thousand Years" represented an impossibility. I asked another girl how that could

---

[13] When I revist this part of the Chinese history, the sound of "lock her up" by the Trump supporters who were against Hillary R. Clinton, and the sound of "Twitter should shut down Trump's account" by the liberal presidential candidate Kamama Harris entered my mind. Is American society more civilized than the China of my youth? We don't really know.

[14] My Grandfather's picture is on the following page.

happen. She swiftly covered my mouth with her hand and told me to shut up. Otherwise, I might be taken to jail or bring trouble to my parents. I could not understand why asking an honest question could be considered a criminal act. That was the first time I came to know everyone was frightened by *something*, although it may differ on a case to case basis.

My Grandfather Clean Life

Then, several of my Father's colleagues, who I usually encountered every day in the street, hung themselves in the Sailor's Club. No one told us why. I still remember one of them was a very handsome middle-aged man, whom we referred to as Uncle Ke. He always greeted me with a big smile on his face. That is, before he was found dangling from the rafters.

My Mom told me that people then had to recite a quote from Mao's Red Book or a praise of Mao before starting any conversation. So, instead of greeting people with "Have you eaten?" people had to say, "*Revolution is not a tea party*, have you eaten[15]?" Or, when a man wanted to buy a steam bun, he had to say things like, "'*Don't ever forget class struggle.*' I want a steam bun." My Mom told me one day she called my Father on the phone to discuss Banyan's health, he answered the phone with: "'*Class struggle is like the rim of a fishing net, once the rope is pulled out, all its mesh open,*' how are you doing?" Then my Mom responded, "'*We have to defeat privatization and criticize revisionism.*' I am fine, but Banyan is sick." If one failed to quote from the Red Book, he or she could be in trouble.

This is how intensively brainwashed our society was. Those effects still vibrate the subconscious today. When keywords are injected into the brain repetitively, they make people believe that the *injected* ideas are their *own* original thinking or belief.

In school, we were taught to love Chairman Mao and the communist party, and we swore to do so. This was based on the teaching that the communist party, led by Mao,

---

[15] "Have you eaten?" means "how are you?" in Chinese custom.

liberated Chinese people from the repression of the Three Mountains: imperialism, feudalism and bureaucracy in collusion with capitalism. We were also told that we were the luckiest children in the world, because we were growing up under the shining aura of the communist party. We were encouraged to study hard, so we would liberate the rest of the people who were still suffering under the repression of the Three Mountains[16].

I enjoyed those liberation stories and their fictive heroes, but wondered why, when all the kids fell in love with Mao and other party heroes, my second brother Banyan was the *exception*. When we played games, everyone wanted the role of a communist party leader or a revolutionary solder. Banyan always wanted to be a high official of the Qiang Kai Shek government, who were characterized as evil guys at that time.

We were told that the Qiang Kai Shek government was incredibly corrupt and repressed its own people, killed numerous communists. Banyan didn't care about any of these teachings. He put cardboard in his cap to mimic Qiang Kai Shek's military figures he had seen from the movies. My parents could not understand why he always wanted to play the evil guy while everyone else wanted to be a communist hero. They always worried that Banyan could continuously bring us trouble. That, he most certainly did.

---

[16] When I revisit this part of the history of China, it reminds me of my Wellesley education that encouraged women to change the world. It resonated with my Childhood education, and I accepted this idea without a second thought. Ten years later, my thinking underwent a foundamental shift. I will tell how and why later.

At the start of my first grade second semester my Grandfather died. I didnot cry, although I missed him. Not because I did not love him, but because I had not built up a strong enough emotional connection with him since we had little interaction. My Mom cried each and every day for over a month after his death. I could not understand why she fought with my Grandfather almost every single day when he was alive, and then cried so hard at his loss. She did not explain the reason until 20 years later.

I hungered so much for knowledge, and received perfect grades each semester for two years, but my parents believed this was as it should be and never complimented me. They fed and clothed me well, and in exchange, I had to study well. If I got an imperfect score on a test like Banyan invariably did, my rear end would get a whipping along with his, with my Mom's tailor-made bamboo switch.

My Father was not a sailor like most of the other parents in my class. My teachers favored students with sailor parents, because sailors could buy commodities cheaper from the countryside for them[17]. For two years, I never had a teacher recommend me as a candidate for captain of the Young Pioneer Team, or any other leadership position. I was the best student, and ambitious to play a more significant role. In fact, I was a natural leader in our adolescent community. About a dozen kids clustered around me whenever I was home. I was very disappointed that my school treated me as invisible.

---

[17] This was in 1975, the 4th year after Dr. Kinger visited China. The peasants were then allowed to sell their products once a month in the free market. So, they could have money to buy products like salt or fabric, and the like.

When the third grade began, we moved to a new home in the Salor's Club by a big swimming pool and a basketball court that sometimes used as a rollerskating rink. One night, I heard my parents chatting about my Father's colleague whose wife was the Principal of another school. I decided to transfer to that school without consulting them. The next day, when I went to school, I confronted my Principal and asked for my transfer papers. He thought it was my parents' decision and gave me the papers.

So, when I brought the papers to my parents, they were shocked, because we had never discussed the matter. However, I just told them I made the decision to transfer because I believed I would do even better in another school. I did not tell them why. That evening, my Father brought me to his colleague's home. His wife welcomed me right away, and I went to her school the next day.

My decision was correct. I was introduced to the class by the Principal. Before they elected a new captain of the Young Pioneer Team, I was recommended as a candidate by the instructor in charge of our class. Since she introduced me as a perfect student, although no one knew me then, all the students voted "yes" for me. School then became much more fun than before, with new activities. I finally had the life I wanted and even made a friend with the girl who shared the same desk with me. Cultural Flood was her name and she lived nearby, so I spent a lot of time at her home because her parents allowed much more freedom than my parents.

Later that year, Banyan secretly begged me to help his transfer to my school, because he was in trouble. Banyan's school shared the same building with the hospital that belonged to the shipping company. One night, he collected the spittoons from all over the hospital, and placed them on the stairway of the school before the students came to evening class.

He then turned off the main power switch of the building when he saw some girl students approaching the staircase. The girls were scared to death when they crashed into the spittoons, and thought they were in the presence of ghosts, because the mortuary was near by. They screamed like bloody murder. This caused complaints not only from the students, but from the hospital as well, because it could not run without power.

This was not Banyan's first mistake. He also broke the school's electricity meter with a basketball and hit several teachers including the vice principal of his school. He knew he was going to be kicked out, and thus begged me for help, because he learned how I accomplished my transfer.

I took Banyan to see my new Principal. She assumed him was as good student as I was, and welcomed him. Soon thereafter, the Principal of his old school called my Father and told him that Banyan had not attended school for a week. When my Father came home, he tied Banyan to his bed and beat him badly with his leather belt.

Banyan got used to be beaten since the age of four. He always managed to do something shocking. When he was only eight, he buried alive a chicken belonging to our neighbor, the police chief. My Mom had to apologize to our neighbor, and bought a new chicken as compensation. Of course, Mom also punished Banyan by not letting him have dinner.

Banyan resented such punishment, and every time when he was told he could not have dinner, he dropped a piece of coal in whatever my Mom was cooking. Coal did not go well with congee. So, he got beaten almost every weekend when my Father was home.

On Sep 9th, 1976, Chairman Mao died. I thought the sky was going to fall since I believed he was the one holding it up for the Chinese people. Though it rained each day for a long time, the sky did not fall.

Many people cried and made paper flower rings for Mao each day. Such activities went on and on for months, and I developed very good handiwork skills. As the captain of the Young Pioneer Team, I did not have to attend class for one week, because I had been guarding Chairman Mao's mourning hall with a red-tasseled spear. Every morning, students and faculties came to the mourning hall to bow to Mao's picture. They looked truly sad and some of them cried. I felt guilty that I was not sad enough to cry.

That year, the school taught us to sing a song:
"The Party, the government, the army, the citizens, the students, east, west, south, north and the middle...the Party leads everything... the always great, honored and correct Party united all the people together... lead us forward."

None of us supposed that a party composed of human beings could sometimes be wrong, since we were brainwashed to always trust the party and treat it as our mother.

Not long after Mao died, the right-wing communists, led by Deng Xiao Ping, swiftly took power from Mao's appointed successors. They then told us that the Cultural Revolution was a mistake made by Mao, and it was over. The government started baby steps of deregulation, and educated elites gradually returned to their posts. People's lives rapidly improved, and became much more free than under Mao. The free market for agricultural products was open everyday, with plenty of choices of food. We could have meat everyday instead of once a week under Mao, but still, no one dared to question why Mao's mistake wasn't the party's mistake. For the most of us, we just blindly trusted that the party was always great, honored and correct.

***

Contrary to the conduct of the naughty Banyan, History was a perfect big brother who always did everything correctly and protected me from Banyan's abuse whenever he could. I do not know whether he ever feared my parents, because he had never been punished. Banyan had always feared my Father and I had always feared my Mom, because it was my Father's job to beat Banyan, and my Mom's job to beat me.

Since I was so afraid of my Mom, I did not tell her that once I was almost drowned in the Yangtze River while trying to save my classmate. In the summer of 1981, I was admitted to Bashu high school. This was an elite high school in Sichuan province, the same school which our future First Lady, Mrs. Hu Jin Tao, attended. Admission to this school was quite an honor at that time, so my Mom promised me that she would not beat me anymore.

Another important occurrence that summer was the flooding of the Yangtze River. Its water reached the street. Many families lost their homes and loved ones in the flood.

When my classmate Cultural Flood[18] heard that we would no longer attend the same school, she invited me to watch the flood together.

So we walked along the river hand-in-hand in the knee-high water, but she fell off a submerged cliff into deep water. No one tried to save her, although thousands of people walked by. I felt I could not leave her alone, and if she had to die, then I would go with her, because she was my best friend and we had set out together on this adventure. I jumped in. Neither of us could swim, and we struggled for what seemed like eternity to reach the shore.

Luckily, I finally clutched a hole in a big stone, which came into sight as the current bore us along. I still had her hand, so I dragged her close to the shore and we climbed, exhausted, to safety. After we got out of the water, I did not dare walk home directly, because I was afraid that Mom would beat me or yell at me on account of my wet and dirty clothes. Until then, Mom *still* washed me and my clothes.

I went to my Father's office building, rinsed myself in the toilet, and went home in the dark. Mom did not notice me, because by 1978, we had moved to a new home, still by the Yangtze River. It had two bedrooms, a living room with our own kitchen and a toilet, which we shared with our neighbor. It was the first time that we didn't have to go to

---

[18] Most people, who were born in mainland China during Mao's time, have names relate to revolution, patriotism or the goal of the communist China. It is important to know this background to understand modern China, because the names became keywords inscribed in people's minds, constantly reminding us the Chinese visions of the world. During those years, very few Chinese families gave their children names like mine.

another building to use the toilet. So, I had my own bedroom for the first time in my life when I was eleven. Before that, I slept in my parents' big bed.

MY HIGH SCHOOL EDUCATION

When the Fall semester of 1981 began, I became a boarder of Bashu High School. I had lots of fun being away from my strict parents and not focusing on studies became my ultimate enjoyment. I took advantage of my Mom's new policy of no further punishment for imperfect grades.

In the first month, a boy from another class named Building China wrote me a love letter and invited a dozen students to picnic in the zoo during National Holidays. I went to the picnic, but did not want to date him, because dating was not allowed in high school and I knew nothing about him. So I wrote him back telling him that both of us should focus on studies and he could be my brother. He accepted this suggestion and we exchanged several letters in the name of sister-brotherhood. We still remain this pure relationship today.

Besides science courses, I enjoyed English the most, because the stories in the text books were much more interesting than the stories in our Chinese or history text books. One of our three English teachers was teacher Chen, almost 70 years old. He spoke in a British accent and taught us several English language songs. One of them was the English version of *La Marseillaise,* a revolutionary song of freedom, and, as I learned later, the French national anthem.

20 years later, when I unconsciously sang this song in front of my American husband Bill, he asked me where I

learned it. I told him that I was taught this song in high school, then he said it was incredible that my high school could teach us an anti-communist song. The truth was, none of us knew this was an anti-communist song except teacher Chen himself!

Then I recalled that another time, teacher Chen came into our classroom with a winter fur hat, a woolen scarf, a long fur coat, a short and thick cotton coat, a woolen sweater... many layers of clothes. After he warmed up, he gradually took off his hat, scarf, long coat...and piled them on the lecture desk. The boy sitting in front of him thought it was funny and said, "Come on, take them all off," then we all laughed out loud. When this happened, our class advisor, teacher Zhou, was secretly monitoring our class through the window. He got angry and broke into the classroom, criticized us for not cherishing and respecting such a wonderful English teacher "that the school had tried so hard to rehabilitate after his miss-treatment in jail."

We were told that teacher Chen was a graduate of Oxford. He came home from the UK to build his motherland in the 50's. However, he did not know telling the truth was dangerous. He criticized Mao's policies when encouraged to do so, then he was jailed until my school desperately needed good English teachers. While he was in jail, he translated all of Mao's Red Books.

I felt sorry that we did not cherish his efforts toward our education and were disrespectful to him. We were too ignorant to understand what he had gone through and did not change our behavior. We continued making noises while he was lecturing us. We were too numb to other people's suffering and could not imagine what freedom means to decent men. We not only disrespected teacher Chen, we behaved the same way to several other eminent teachers who had gone through the similar tragedies during the Cultural Revolution.

During the next two years, my grades dropped as a result of having too much fun. My class advisor, teacher Zhou, visited my parents at our third new home. We moved to this home in Jan 1982. It had two bigger bedrooms, two patios, a kitchen with natural gas supply and its own toilet. This was a first.

The right-wing led government's deregulation constantly sped up economic development. During Mao's time, our family lived in the same home for over ten years. After he died, we moved four times in nine years. Every time, we moved to a better and bigger home.

By this time, my brothers had gone to college and moved out. When our class advisor Zhou found out that I had a big bedroom, yet was crowded in with nineteen other students in one dorm, he asked my parents to take me home. Thereafter, I had to take early morning buses to go to school with no more lazy morning sleep.

Although I was still angry with teacher Zhou for deporting me, I had lots of fun commuting. I am grateful now for his vision of great potential in me. I could not understand his intentions then. He was indeed a loving and dedicated teacher.

Our new home was still on the tip of the peninsula formed by Yangtze and Jialin Rivers. I had to rise every morning at 6:30 am and walk down the street to take a bus since the school started at 7:15 am. The most impressive thing to me was the crowds.

There were always endless lines of people who had to catch the buses during rush hour. To be able to get to school on time, I learned how to squeeze myself into an already very crowded bus. I used to bet with the School Flower[19] that I could catch any bus I wanted, because I did not care how I looked. She had to whip herself into perfect shape all the time, so she would rather miss a bus and be late for class than look all disheveled from squeezing onto a bus.

However, sometimes, I did regret my techniques for penetrating super crowded buses, because I could not even give my small nose enough space to breath. One day, I boarded a bus as the last passenger and the weight of the door closing squeezed me in. I found my hair in a crazy mess, my hands gripped the door like a lizard on a wall, and my nose squashed out of shape against it. I could not breathe, which didn't matter because I would only inhale a lot of CO_2 expelled by my fellow passengers. This was extremely uncomfortable during the summer heat, because some people smelled. Other times, men pushed against girls in obscene ways.

One morning, I saw a very good-looking boy, ten years or younger, fall from a moving bus, the back wheel of which ran over one of his legs. I was surprised that the young boy did not cry but stared at the huge hole opening on his leg. Two adults carried him away to the hospital. I remember the skin of his leg opening like a window in a wall. I could see the red flesh and blood vessels in his leg. This image has stayed with me forever, and I always wonder why his parents

---

[19] School Flower was the most beautiful and popular girl in our school and my new best friend in the class.

let him take buses to school - unaccompanied - when he was so young.

At times other than rush hour, I used to take a bus and travel all over the city for entertainment with my best friend, the School Flower. It was just so much fun watching people doing things in the city; this also gave me a chance to learn the names of the streets.

Because of my inability to adapt to the changes of my life, such as having to get up early every morning, I resented our class advisor Zhou. I made a stupid mistake I shall regret forever. I gave him a bad nickname and wrote it in big letters on the blackboard. He was offended and angry when he saw it. He invited my Mom to the school to have a chat.

During my first two years, my Mom had only gone to the school once to bring me a quilt for the approaching cold weather. When I told my Mom she had to meet teacher Zhou, she could not believe it. She thought only naughty boy students precipitated parent meetings. She felt ashamed and refused to go. I told her if she would not go, then I wouldn't be admitted to class. So she had to go, and she apologized to teacher Zhou for me. Later, I felt deeply sorry for what I had done to him, so I went to see him at his home several times after graduating from Bashu High School.

Although I did not pay much attention to my studies, my grades were not terribly bad due to my solid foundation. However, my confidence was seriously damaged by my scores from the college entrance test in 1984. The Chinese educational system provides only one chance each year for college entrance exams. If you blow it, you must wait for another year.

When I encountered a problem in the math section I could not solve, I didn't abandon that problem and continue with the rest of the test. Therefore, I screwed up the whole section. I was so upset because I knew I could not get into any school I wanted with that math grade. So I was not in the mood to take the rest of the tests. My Mom observed me avoiding the remainder of the tests, so she took out her tailor-made bamboo switch, that had not been used for years, and beat me. Thereafter, I went, but was in no mood to do my best.

The result was not a surprise to me. I begged my Mom to give me another chance, and promised I would go to the best college in China if she gave me another chance. She rejected this idea, because the elite high school I had attended required one extra year of education than ordinary high schools. She thought she had already fed me for one more year than the other kids, and I should, therefore, be on my own.

I felt I was a failure and had no desire to face my classmates for many years. The problem eventually resolved itself at our 20th anniversary reunion in 2004. Once we got together again, we no longer wanted to be apart. Even today, we still daily talk on social media, just like a big family. In fact, I speak to them and have dinners with them more often than with my own family members. Later, after I got married, my classmates hosted a welcoming party for my husband Bill. He was so impressed that 60 of them showed up. He wondered how we could keep such a tight friendship for so long.

Me & the School Flower Ya Hong

MY MOM

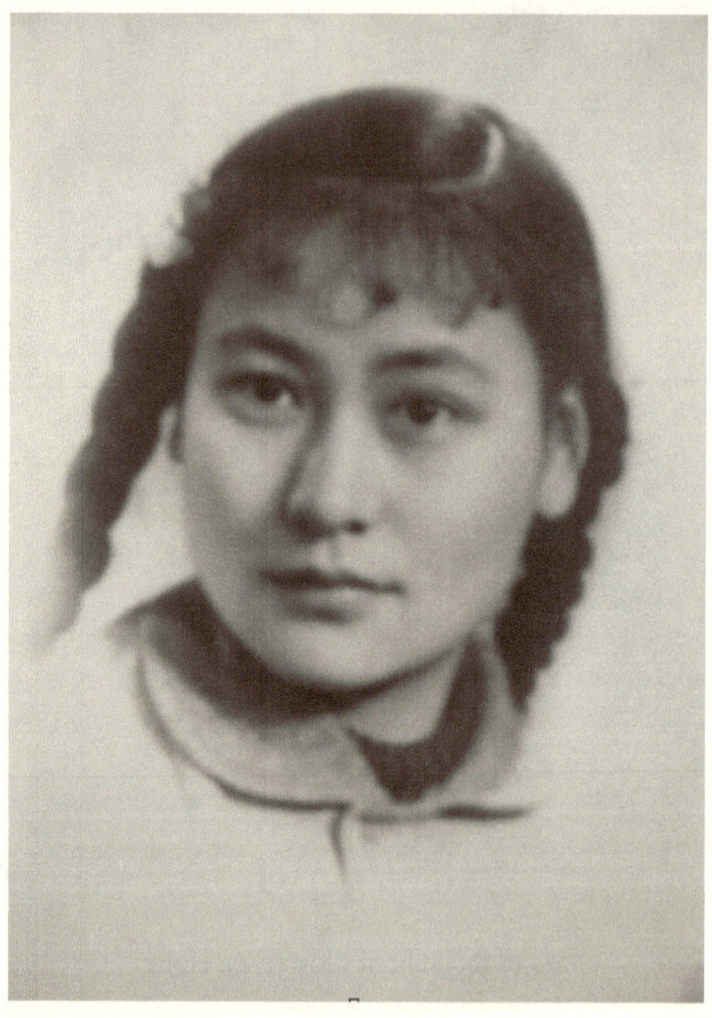

MY MOM

My Mom's name is Rich and Kind. Although she has never been rich materially, she is rich in spirit. She is always kind to the unfortunate.

I had very little communication with either of my parents when I was young. I did not understand why, until the political atmosphere became much more relaxed. I used to tell my Mom that if my maternal Grandfather was still alive, I would spoil him with lots of love, unlike how she treated him before he died. This sounded like criticism to my Mom, and she always reacted: "You don't know anything, you have no right to say that." My Mom is not a person you can force to reveal what she does not want to tell. So, I lived with this puzzle until I became mature enough, at least in my Mom's eyes, to be given an answer to this mystery.

My Mom is very reserved. I am different than her. I say what I mean and mean what I say. This bothers her a lot, because she thought that some day, my bold mouth might cause trouble, because in an environment that has no freedom of speech, wagging tongues can strangle a person when the Sky[20] changes. During her life, the political skies over China have changed multiple times.

I worked in government owned businesses since 1984, then quit in 1992 and became a successful business woman working for a Hong Kong commercial kitchen equipment company. In 1994, before I was 27, I bought a big condominium in a 35-floor high rise in the center of the richest city in China, Shenzhen, Hong Kong's neighbor. I would

---

[20] The Sky is my Mom's metaphor for political atmosphere, because in ancient China, the emperor was called "the son of the sky" or "the son of the heaven." Most Chinese people consider politics is only the business of the government and has nothing to do with citizens.

fly my parents to Shenzhen every year to spend time with me. During the years in my new condo, one day I criticized the local police chief didn't try his best to save a girl's life. My Mom fearfully told me to shut up.

I naively reacted to her: "There's nothing to be afraid of, China is open to the world and it will never close again." She didn't believe me and asked me with doubt in her voice: "Are you sure?"

As ignorant as I was, I assured her, I explained: "The Chinese people supported the communist revolution because they had a bad life. 80% of the population were uneducated and illiterate before 1949, and they had never known a normal life. Now people are educated and enjoying some freedom, they will only want more rather than less of what is becoming precious to them."

My communist education had provided us a poem:

> *'Life is precious,*
> *love worth more,*
> *for the sake of freedom,*
> *both can be abandoned.*
> *- Petogfi Sandor'"*

My beautiful middle-aged Mom blinked her big shining eyes, and mysteriously asked:
"Do you want to know why I always fought with your Grandfather when you were little?"
"Why? I thought you just had a bad temper and got angry easily."
"You do not know about a lot of things. I did not tell you because I was afraid that you would say something to the

others who would cause trouble for our family. You are so innocent, and everybody is a good and beautiful person in your eyes."

"Everyone Is so nice to me though."

"Not really. Some of them just pretended to be nice to you, because your Father was a respected executive in the company."

She was referring to our neighbors and our old colleagues in the shipping company. My parents always lived in compounds with neighbors who worked in the same shipping company, because that was the norm in the old communist system. Housing was provided by the company for which one worked. Now, government-owned companies no longer provide housing. Instead, people have free choice to buy wherever they like.

"I don't understand," I responded.

"Do you remember our old neighbor, Aunt Xing?"

"Yes, what about her?"

"Aunt Xing once told me that she was given a mission to spy on us by the Revolutionary Committee."

"She had been your best friend!"

"Yes, that's why she later told me the truth. She was told to make friends with me and get information to report to the Revolutionary Committee."

"Well, she did not have much to report."

"That is why I shut up my mouth, because we *did* have something to hide."

"Weird, what could that be?"

"Your Grandfather. He did not behave like an ordinary clerk. He had a rich man's look and style, so people suspected him."

"I thought he was just a bank clerk."

"It was not that simple! And we had relatives in Taiwan and the U.S. Do you remember when you were in high school, my niece Yong Lian visited us?"

"Yes, *that* was weird too, because I had never known you had such a relative until her visit. I thought we had no relatives except Wang Yu Li and her mother, who live in down town Chongqing!"

"Wang Yu Li is from my grandmother's side. Yong Lian is from my grandfather's side, we used to play together when we were little. Then, when the Chiang Kai Shek government failed and fled to Taiwan, both her parents and elder brothers got on the plane and left her with her wet nurse. Then the wet nurse took her to the countryside where she came from, and raised her."

"So we have relatives in Taiwan?"

"Yes, lots of them. Some of them immigrated to the U.S. in the 70's. They were well educated people, could have been successful anywhere. Yong Lian visited us, because her mom, who was living in Taiwan, wanted to find a way to come to mainland China, and sent her a letter through a friend in Hong Kong."

"So *this* was why you were so angry with Grandpa? I still do not understand."

"It is much more than that."

So, my Mom told me about her unusual childhood. She was born in 1938, the year of the Tiger, and the second year of the 8 year long anti-Japanese War. She remembered the dark gray bombers flying overhead almost every day when she was little, because Chongqing was the temporary capital of the Chiang Kai Shek government.

During those times, people didn't know whether they would be killed by bombs that day or the next, so the rich just wined and dined, attended ballroom dances, gambled and smoked opium. My Mom's beautiful mother married my Grandfather Clean Life who was from a good family, well educated, and very handsome. Their marriage was almost perfect, and their first child was my Mom's elder brother, Bull. My Mom followed thereafter.

When she was very little, my mother's mother contracted *menolipsis*, a kind of sickness that ended menstruation prematurely. She died when my Mom was just two years old. My Grandfather was very depressed, because he believed it was his fault since he didn't take good care of my Grandmother due to his spoiled, self-centered lifestyle. One relative told us my Grandfather had two maids caring for him since he learned to walk, one to play with him, the other to carry an extra set of clothes just in case the first became soiled.

Later, my Mom's elder brother Bull[21] also died due to some strange undiagnosed illness. Then, my Grandfather betrayed his name, Clean Life, by becoming addicted to opium. So this superstitious family presumed it was my Mom's fault, because she was born in a Tiger year. They thought her overly strong life force might threaten all the weaker members of the family. Since then, my Mom was informally given to a relative's family and only allowed to call her own father "Great Uncle," instead of "Papa," as do ordinary kids. She also had to address all her real family members as if they were just acquaintances.

---

[21] Bull as in the bovine, not bull as in excrement.

When my Mom revealed this, it reminded me that when my Grandfather died, the neighbors who came to comfort her asked me why my Mom called her own Father "Great Uncle" instead of "Papa." I did not know the answer, so did not give one. However, the recollection of her calling: "Great Uncle! Great Uncle! Wake up, it's your lunch time. You like Dan Dan noodles, here you are!" was so vivid. On this occasion, after she failed to rouse my Grandfather, she asked me to wake him up. I tried many times, but without success. I did not know he was already dead and went to school.

When I returned in the afternoon, a neighbor told me that my Grandfather died - and that my Mom was hysterical. I could not believe it. I imagined he had woken up and eaten his noodles. I just could not believe how someone could look fine the day before, and then fall asleep and never wake up.

In fact, my Mom was excluded from her family since the age of two. After that, she barely saw her father and was told that he had gone to work in Tianjin for her uncle, who was her father's eldest brother and a powerful man in the Chiang Kai Shek government. So, she either stayed at relatives' homes or stayed home alone like an orphan. The rich relatives had numerous kids and grandkids, wet nurses and maids. Their parents were so busy working, dancing, playing ma jiang, wining and dining that they did not even have time for their own kids. I could only imagine how little attention my Mom received. She told me that no one noticed she was old enough to go to school, so she did not get an education until the communists seized power and required all citizens to learn to read.

MY MOM

My Mom told me that my Grandfather disappeared during the anti-Japanese War and Civil War. Then he showed up when she was already working for an Army Hospital. This was in 1955 when she was 17. He asked about her life. She told him she had a handsome boyfriend who was a doctor at the hospital.

However, my Grandfather told her he was not a good choice because this man had too much education, and would not treasure her as she deserved. Then he introduced my Father to her and told her that my Father was working for the biggest company in Chongqing and a party official. This meant 'good protection' to people like my Grandfather, who came from a former rich, but now threatened family.

My Mom did not agree because she was in love with the doctor. My Grandfather pushed her to marry my Father because the political situation was growing serious. My Mom saw some of her classmates' fathers or relatives shot in public because they were capitalists or landlords. She was accordingly scared and married my Father, whom she did not love at all. They had nothing in common. My Mom grew up in a big city, whereas my Father's parents were fallen landlords. He grew up in the countryside of Hunan province. She cried immediately after their wedding, because she did not like this geeky tall, spectacled guy.

Another reason why my Mom so resented my Grandfather was because he hid the doctor's love letters to my Mom for her own good. My Mom found out the truth after my Grandfather moved in with my parents. I saw the handsome boyfriend's photo many times later, and was amazed that my Father was never jealous of him.

In fact, my Grandfather had been waiting for the Chiang Kai Shek government to retaliate against mainland China. He did not want to work for the communist government. So he got married again and had another daughter, lived on selling his personal possessions during the years after the communist takeover. Then the new wife divorced him. I only saw the daughter from this marriage, Mass[22], twice in my life. Once was when she needed to find a job and importuned my Father; the second time was at my Grandfather's funeral. In fact, I did not realize she was my Mom's half sister, since she was just a few years older than my eldest brother History. Mass's mom, Wise, was a high school teacher in Nan Kai High School, an elite high school in Chongqing. She was an elegant, middle aged woman when I saw her, at least 30 years younger than my Grandfather.

So, my Mom concluded that another reason why my Grandfather pushed her to marry my Father was that my Grandfather's marriage was in trouble. He was seeking someone kind enough to protect him both politically and economically. Mom felt she was betrayed and resented her father.

Mom explained the reason why she fought with my Grandfather so often was because he was not careful about his behavior. He still kept his identification issued by the old government, and daydreamed it would return. This could have caused my Father to lose his position and the whole family to be sent to live in the countryside, which my Mom thought was a terrible idea. She believed that it could grow

---

[22] Mass for people, not the mass for physics.

even worse. She saw her classmate, a very beautiful young girl at age 10, witnessed the execution of her own father, on stage, in front of the public, due to his association in the old government.

Then, I remembered when I first started to attend school, when we criticized Lin and Kong[23], my Grandfather used to complain to my Mom: "Look at what Wang Yun Song[24] did to this country! He educated two future vice premiers[25] and sent them to France, how did they reward him? They destroyed our ancestor's thousand-year heritage!" Yes, my Grandpa did sound very anti-revolutionary, but who was Wang Yun Song? I did not get the answer to this question until my last year of high school.

Mom's cousin Wang Yu Li, who was a very good seamstress, lived in downtown Chongqing with her mom in her grandfather Wang Yun Song's house after he died in 1958. My Mom used to buy some fabric for me and let me bring to Wang Yu Li to fashion shirts and dresses.

One day during my last semester of high school, I brought a piece of new fabric to Wang Yu Li to make a dress, and she told me that she was writing to Deng Xiao Ping, because her legs suffered an affliction which went untreated during to the imprisonment of Deng Xiao Ping. I thought it

---

[23] Kong - Confucious
[24] Wang Yun Song is my Great Granduncle who was a high official in the Qing Dynasty and Chairman of the chamber of commerce in Chongqing before China became communist. He was also a successful business man. Wang Yu Li is Wang Yun Song's granddaughter, my Mom's cousin.
[25] These two were Deng Xiao Ping and Nie Rong Zheng, the future vice premieres of China. They joined the communist revolution in France and brought back their leadership experiences and ideology to China.

was ridiculous that she thought Deng Xiao Ping would care about her legs. Surprisingly, when I returned to her home to pick up my dress, Wang Yu Li showed me a brand-new wheelchair with real leather fittings, and she told me it was sent with a letter from Deng Xiao Ping. I brought this big news back to my Mom.

Mom heard this and was excited: "Great! So, Deng Xiao Ping does remember my Granduncle. 'Great Uncle'(her father) did not believe that the communist party could still remember my Granduncle's contribution."
"What contribution?"
"My Granduncle, Wang Yun Song, was a high official in Qing Dynasty, and he became a very successful business man later on when the Republic of China was established. He was the Chairman of the Chamber of Commerce in Chongqing.
"He founded a non-profit school and sent 100+ of his best students to France. He covered everything, paid for their passports, travel fees, and gave them lots of silver dollars . . . but I bet, when he sent them to France, he did not realize that two of them would overthrow the government and become vice premiers of China.
"'Great Uncle' resented Granduncle, because he believed that Granduncle nurtured these communists who later turned China upside down and broke his family apart."

After knowing my Mom's true background, I felt sorry for her and began to understand that her improper behavior in the past was due to an unusual childhood and its political environment. She was not a mean person but a victim of Chinese history and tradition. Since then, I always try to spoil her with a lot of love, as my Father did.

MY FATHER

My beloved Father's name is Together. He was born in 1931. My Father's Grandfather's family were successful merchants. When they visited the town of Zhang Jia Jie, in Hunan, they thought the place was as beautiful as heaven, because it was so fertile and cheap. They bought a big piece of it for settlement by my Father's grandfather and his brother.

Chinese families liked to have many children, and each of the two brothers had more than ten children and a lot of grandchildren. My Father was the third child and the first son of his parents, who had thirteen children. I have never met my paternal grandparents and only heard about them from my Father. From what I have heard, my Father never liked his life in his hometown. He said that his parents' generation was totally spoiled and rotten, did not work at all, but gambled and smoked opium every day.

Opium, a confection of colonialism, sounds like a normal consumer good consumed by my Grandfather's generation in China. Though living in different provinces, both of my Grandfathers were victims of opium. Understanding the role of opium is key to understanding the evolution of China.

Father used to tell me that my Grandfather had inherited such a big piece of land that if a horseman galloped in one direction for a week, the horse would be still cosuming grass on that land. However, no one took care of the land. It was leased out, but my Father's family often forgot to collect the rent. Or, tragically, they would gamble away pieces of this land. Although regarded to be a bad thing at the time, it turned out to be a benefit later. By the time the communist took over the country in 1949, due to mismanagement of the

MY FATHER

land and loss of it by gambling, my Father's parents did not have enough to qualify as landlords, since what remained was dispersed among so many kids and grand kids. Therefore, they were categorized as rich peasants, a much safer classification than landlords.

At least, they were not murdered like some of the big landlords. Their family was not branded with that disreputable identification, landlord, which would adversely affect the future of their offsprings. For example, my Father would not otherwise have the chance to go to the Army school and became a party leader. A categorization of one's parents or grandparents as landlords was considered seriously bad when I was young.

When the Army School came to recruit on my Father's campus, in order to escape from his corrupt family life style, and follow his ambition to build a communist China, he joined the Liberation Army without consulting his parents. They were busy playing mahjong and did not care anyway. So my Father studied telecommunications in the Liberation Army's Midsouth Telecommunication Technology School in Wuhan, Hubei province. After graduation, he was sent to work for the Yangtze Shipping Company's branch in Yichang, Hubei province.

My Father has always been a doer rather than a talker. He spoke little but worked very hard, both at home and at his company. By the time he met my Mom in 1958, he was 27. This was considered too old to be single during those times, but he was accomplished educationally and career-wise. So people around him enthusiastically helped him to find a wife. I don't know how my maternal Grandfather got to know my Father, but he was sharp enough to identify my Father's almost flawless personality, which would guarantee a stable life for my Mom.

When my Father met my Mom, he found her so beautiful he had no reservation about devoting the rest of his life to make her happy. Unfortunately, my Mom did not appreciate his kindness and love. She confessed to him that she just used the relationship for protection. She could not believe she had to abandon her dream life with the doctor, forever. My Father assured her repeatedly that she and her family would be safe, since he would defend them with his life and love. He proved true to his word.

My Mom did not give up easily. She fought with my Father repeatedly which annoyed him. He consulted his mentor about how he should deal with such a situation, since he could not focus on work. His kind and wise mentor advised him to ignore her and focus on work, when my Mom was absorbed with two or three children, she would no longer fight with him. This proved to be true. When the political atmosphere grew more serious, they no longer fought but bonded together to survive.

Endless political power struggles took my Father away from Chongqing three times. No matter whether the change was a promotion or demotion, my Father always fought his way back to Chongqing to be with my Mom, he kept his promise to protect my Mom and our family.

He was so protective he spoiled all of us, especially my Mom. As a professional housewife, my Mom never strayed beyond our own gate. My Father purchased all the food. Every morning, he rose at 5:30 am to buy fresh vegetables and meat, along with our breakfast, then helped the janitor clean his office and fill thermos bottles for the rest of the offices. My Father turned over 100% of his income to my Mom and he had no right to decide how money should be spent, and took only direct orders from her. Not only that, he always humbly awaited criticism by my Mom concerning the work he had done for our family.

Even as a youngster, I felt my Mom was too bossy, and concluded that I would not be that kind of woman when I grow up. I would give my man 100% respect, allow him the right to make stupid decisions, and to indulge himself every so often[26]. My Mom behaved like she was the queen of the house and imposed her rules that all must obey without further discussion. I believe her confidence came from my Father's unconditional love and pampering, because he knew that my Mom had been bereft of love from infancy. My Father never told us that he loved us, but he expressed his deep love through solid action over time.

My Father has been an honest, dedicated career and family man. All our family members, friends, and relatives speak with great respect and admiration about my Father. In 1984, my Mom's friend Mr. Lu and his powerful relatives from Taiwan, visited our home and expressed his sincere respect of my Father in front our family. He said, "It is incredible that you are such a clean official when corruption is everywhere." Yes, my Father is a true communist who believes in dedication and honesty instead of abusive monopoly power. His conduct and reputation are one of the great

---

[26] My American husband concedes I am, in this regard, an expert. However, this overgiving feature turned out to be very bad for it spoiled all of my love relationships. Later, I found it interesting that overgiving is also a feature of socialism.

heritages of my generation, and we would all be rewarded if we emulated and cherished his values.

CRUISING ON THE YANGTZE

THE M.S. BASHAN

In December 1984, I joined the largest company in town, the Yangtze Shipping Company, at which my Father and brothers worked. Since I was the top performer on the entrance tests and had the height and looks required, I had the best chance to work on a brandnew luxury cruise ship, M.S. Ba Shan, cruising the Yangtze River. Many people coveted this job, even my brothers were jealous of me, because History was working in an office on shore as a telecommunication engineer and Banyan was a telegraph operator on a cargo boat. I would work on a beautiful cruise ship and travel to beautiful places for free.

M.S. Ba Shan was chartered by a Swedish American company, Lind Bladt & Co. It was an extremely beautiful and luxurious vessel, even in Westerners' eyes. That was why our central government always picked it to entertain our most important Western guests.

The boat was 84 meters long and 27 meters wide, with the hull and super structure painted white with pink trim. The rotunda of the ball room was painted in hues of blue, yellow, white and red. It had five decks. The first deck contained the lower portion of the engine room; the second was staff housing, more engine room, a laudry room and kitchen; the third deck was devoted to senior staff member cabins and passenger cabins; the fourth contained only suites, but also had a large elegant dining room, a recreation room, a centrally located clinic and a stylish sightseeing lounge in the bow next to the presidential suites; on the fifth deck was a big ball room, a swimming pool outside of the ballroom, and captain and commissar suites. Above the fifth deck was a sightseeing tower. I still remember the large decorative fan on the wall of the ballroom bar, with two smaller fans on either side of the lounge wall in front of the swimming pool.

We had more than 120 staff members and 4-5 American executives, but usually, we had no more than 12~38 prestigious guests. When guests arrived at the dock, the sailors' orchestra, all dressed in white uniforms, would play Chinese music to welcome them on board. The next morning, when the boat set sail, the sailors' orchestra would play Auld Lang Syne on the dock. Also, when the boat reached its destination, another sailors' orchestra would be on the dock playing music to welcome our guests again.

MY EDUCATION IN ECONOMICS BEGINS

During my first year working on M.S. Ba Shan, it hosted an important conference, which not only changed China, but also the geopolitical course of the world[27]. In the

---

[27] In my view, this was the critical point that consolidated China's rise and accelerated America's fall, because, at this point, the Chinese leadership honestly and humbly admitted they needed to learn everything about economic development from the west, and western world leaders freely gave them their most precious wisdom - Reaganomics. China married this wisdom to its ancient philosophy, strongly and consistently implemented it for 35 years while America abandoned it

seminal year of 1985, the first *International Macroeconomics and Management Forum*, was held on our boat during Sep 2nd through the 9th.

The central government could not find a better place than our boat to host our precious western guests, the world's top economists. The guests included 1981 Nobel Prize laureate *Professor James Tobin* from Yale University, and *Professor Alexander Cairncross* from Cambridge University. Economists and leaders from all over the world were invited to have discussions with our top Chinese economists, including *Xue Mu Qiao* and *Wu Jing Lian*, Chinese central government leaders, such as *Xiang Huai Cheng* and *Ma Hong* also attended.

The government-owned media now records the fact that this conference instructed China how to transform from a planned economy to a market economy. The attendees focused on "government-market-businesses," and prepared theoretical approaches for the framework of the 13th People's Delegation Conference in 1987. Meaning, the government could adjust the market, and the market would direct business.

Today, many top Chinese economists believe that people cannot exaggerate the true impact that this event had on China. If you Google "M.S. Ba Shan Conference" in Mandarin, you will get numerous results. Many of them were written for the 20th anniversary of this event, because the attendees still have vivid memories concerning it. Some of them believe that this was the only real international

---

and played the 'big government' game that had been proven wrong by both China and the USSR.

macroeconomic forum in Chinese history. Others claim that China needs another "M.S. Ba Shan Conference", today!

The year 1985 represented an important turning point for China. That year, the government started to formally open a portion of the market for fish, eggs, poultry and some other goods. These were baby steps. This means local consumers began to be able to buy some goods without ration tickets. Before, our purchases of almost everything was rationed, and ration tickets were traded in the black market. However, due to the lack of application of proper economic theories, the growth of GDP in that year was 12%, much less than the growth of money supply at 25.3%. Under these conditions, China almost had a bank run because people did not know if prices of goods would stop increasing.

Years later, some of the participants of the meeting pointed out that although the government determined to engage in economic reform, it did not know what to proceed. How could inflation be curbed? That would normally be the job of a central bank, and China did not have one. It only had the People's Bank, a commercial bank which acted as the central bank. So, the central government invited preeminent economists from the West to seek guidance. As a result, they learned a lot, according to Xin Hua News agency reports at the time.

On the evening of Sep 1st, 1985, our captain hosted a welcoming cocktail party in the ballroom for all our guests. On the morning of Sep 2nd, 1985, the 80-year-old Chinese economist, *Mr. Xue Mu Qiao*, announced the opening of the forum. During the first two days, due to language barriers and conceptual differences between the West and the East, the parties could not get along. Then, *Mr. Lin Chong Gen,* who was the first director of the Chinese Office of the World Bank, helped bridge communications. He was born in Taiwan, could speak both Chinese and English well, and understood Chinese customs and traditions. His sophisticated social skills and expertise promoted the efficacy of the forum.

Our western guests spoke of the price of labor, labor markets, goods markets, financial markets and production factor markets. For many of the Chinese attendees, it was the first time in their lives to hear the concept that wages are the prices of labor. They could not believe their ears, because the *selling* of labor was not considered reputable, since the essence of communism was the *contribution* of labor to build a prosperous country. It was also the first time they learned the government could indirectly cool or heat the economy by adjusting the interest rate.

Xin Hua news agency stated, years later, that this forum helped the government establish a framework for further economic reform, to wit, promotion of Reaganomics in a market economy. However, change *then* was not as easy as it might appear *in retrospect*. The central government believed the public was not ready to accept the concept of a market economy, due to the longtime persistent promotion and educational inculcation of a socialist-planned economy. If the term 'market economy' was mentioned too soon, the Maoists might want to fight to eradicate capitalist roots again. So, it was suggested *not* to call it a market economy but instead a *commodity* economy. Later, people described this change as 'switching on the left turn signal, but driving into the right lane.'

The Chinese attendees appreciated the input of the Western experts, and they praised them as most honorable and sincere in their efforts to help China's economic reform. A remarkable number of the young Chinese attendees later were promoted to important government offices. Among them were:

Xiang Huai Cheng the future minister of the Treasury Department;

Lou Ji Wei the future vice minister of the Treasury Department;

Guo Shu Qing the future governor of Shan Dong province, then the Chairman of Security Exchange Commission;

Hong Hu, the future governor of Ji Ling province;

Zhang Wei Ying, the future dean of Guang Hua school of Beijing University and a prominent economist in China.

The Chinese had a tradition of mixing business with pleasure, the latter including sightseeing, wining and dining, and other entertaining programs. I remember a Western guest complaining to me he was invited for a business meeting on the boat, and he wondered why his Chinese hosts pushed him sightsee on shore every day, during working hours. I thought then he must have been too serious about work. After having studied economics, now I surmise he might have been so attached to the subject of his expertise that he could not have fun while unsolved puzzles nibbled at his mind. However, despite differing cultural nuances, it seemed to me that everyone believed the forum achieved great success.

During the evening of Sep 8th, 1985, our captain hosted a farewell banquet and a party for our guests. He suggested that I sing an English song for our precious guests, and I did. Now I am grateful for having such wonderful memory of this historical event.

One of the guests was Li Miao, who was Chairman Mao's translator and could speak in different English accents. Though his English was thought to be perfect, I still heard people complain about his trouble translating buzz words for experts at such a professional forum, because he was never trained in economics. I could only appreciate this complaint 24 years later when I encountered economic buzz words at Wellesley. Indeed, although my husband is an American lawyer and has an honor's degree in English from Berkeley, when asked by me to explain buzz words in my economics textbook, he begged me to desist, because it was not English to him!

I really liked our guests. So even though I was shy, I sang the song, *Take Me Home, Country Road*[28], by the late singer John Denver, for our guests at the farewell party. It was the first time in my life that I sang in front of such a large group of Western people. After that, I sang that song at *every* farewell party *every* weekend until I left the boat.

MY ABORTED FIRST LOVE

A handsome young magician caught my attention at that farewell party. 'Celebrating China' was an intern commissar on our boat. He had a square face with a dimple on the right side, a pair of big shining round eyes, beautiful straight white teeth as one sees in toothpaste ads, an athletic body, neither too tall, nor too short. When he forgot to shave, his beard grew and that looked charming to me. Whenever

---

[28] See the first picture on page 74.

he saw me, a big smile appeared on his face. I thought: he might like me.

So, I included visits to his cabin[29] many times in my social rounds during his one-month internship on our boat. I learned that he had beautiful handwriting and calligraphy, could build and play several Chinese instruments, and had talents as a carpenter, tailor, silversmith and cook. I could not imagine anything he could not do, so I was fascinated. Then, when his internship lapsed and he left our boat, I felt a kind of emptiness, but did not know why.

Later, my Mom visited me on shipboard, and asked me whether there was any crew member pursuing me. "No," I said. Not satisfied, she inquired whether there were crew members pursuing the other five female shipmates who attended my English training class and came on board with me. I responded, "Yes, each had several suitors."

Of course, the company had picked the most beautiful girls from thousands of candidates. Tall and beautiful were the important criteria, not English proficiency. Mom worried that I might not know how to catch a boyfriend, so she asked, again, whether there was anyone on my boat I liked. I told her there *was* one, but, unfortunately, he was gone, forever. Mom extracted his name from me and left.

A few months passed by while our boat docked with the other cruise ships at the shipyard for maintenance. We had ballroom dancing for the crew every night. During these times, we had no work to do and could socialize with personnel from other boats. Ballroom dancing had just been

---

[29] Celebrating China was sharing a cabin with three other crew members.

CRUISING ON THE YANGTZE

revived as a cultural nuance of economic reform and development. Like birds during spring, people began to dress in different colors and styles, in contrast to the drab colors and unisex styles which emulated military dress under Mao. Surprisingly, Celebrating China appeared and invited me to visit his boat which was docked nearby.

His vessel was a passenger boat carrying many peasants. When I came aboard, crowds of people gaped at me as though I were a movie star, because they saw me dressed in a beautiful cruise ship uniform and giving directions to a foreigner in English. At that time, it was rare to see westerners from any passenger boat, because they usually stayed in the higher-class cabins and were segregated from the Chinese passengers.

Celebrating China told me that my Mom visited him and asked him to be my boyfriend. I was stunned, but glad. We set a date to meet each other at the sand beach by the Yangtze River in that evening. I was so excited to go on this date and thought we had much to discuss. However, when I met him at the beach, to my great disappointment, he did not say anything other than to invite me to sit down on a big pebble stone, and tried to kiss me. I was not prepared for this to occur. It did not follow any procedure of love stories I had read. So, I was scared, stood up, and ran away from him.

Since then, I wondered whether Celebrating China intended to marry me although we never had a meaningful date. Whenever I have seen a fortune teller, I paid to discover this answer. Though I might have coughed up ten separate fees, not one of them told me I would end up with him. One fortune teller told me firmly it would have been impossible for me to marry him, but I would have my own successful career. I could not believe all these prophecies, because I thought, as long as I behaved as a good woman, Celebrating China would cherish me.

After my abortive date with Celebriting China, I did not see him for almost a year, but missed him every day, and imagined, constantly, what he might be doing. I wrote him numerous love letters expressing how much I admired him. Then he appeared on my boat to visit a colleague but ended up leaving the boat with me. He invited me to have dinner with his family. After dinner, while walking me back to my boat, he brought up the issue of having a baby. That scared me again since I was only 19, had no experience with men, never kissed, nor had sex. So, I swiftly ran away from him a second time.

After that, he never came to my boat again and I missed him very much. So I asked my Father to put me on the temporary replacement team for passenger boats, because, in this way, I might have a chance to work on Celebrating China's boat, which was the ugliest and smallest passenger boat on the Yangtze River. Many people could not understand why I left the luxury cruise ship for passenger boats. Only my parents knew it was in pursuit of love.

I worked on a different boat almost every two weeks, but I was never sent to work on Celebrating China's boat. Perhaps, the HR office did not believe that I should work on an old boat like that since it was a huge come down from the luxury liner on the Yangtze. Thus, I found excuses to take his boat from time to time, so I could see him and talk to him. Whenever I encountered him again, he always showed hospitality and respect, but no longer touched me.

Then I was sent to work as a librarian on a passenger boat. The captain and the commissar liked me. They asked me to stay on their boat and promised to let me take one month paid leave every other two months. I thought this was a rare and great offer, so I accepted.

I had fun both on or off the boat. Sitting at the library every day and reading lots of books that I did not need to buy was an easy job. When I got bored, I practiced calligraphy on old newspapers, or organized ballroom dancing parties for the staff and passengers in the evenings. My library was the only air-conditioned place on the boat, and the ceiling was decorated with colorful lights that changed with music. I met many interesting people there, from government officials to business people, westerners from all over the world. When off the boat, I enrolled in a school to take computer science courses and earned a professional certificate. Or, I deliberately took Celebrating China's boat for fun, since there was no cost for sailors to take other boats. I just needed to flash my working ID. However, in the realm of romance, no progress was made.

I WAS DEMOTED A PUBLIC TOILET CLEANER

Later, a bad thing happened to me. After I finished my one-month vacation and got back to my boat, the captain was sent to another passenger boat; the commissar was promoted to work on my former cruise ship, M.S. Bashan; and the manager of the service department went off duty, staying at his home far away in the countryside. The new manager of the service department had not seen me for one month. When I returned, he told me that my vacation privileges were unreasonable. No librarian on the Yangtze River had one third of a year off except me, all other librarians had only 52 days off per year. He was angry both at me and the leaders who offered this benefit.

So he demoted me to work as a stewardess for the passenger cabins. On this type of boat, the highest class of cabins was second class, and it was to this realm I was demoted. But since I was demoted, I thought, 'why don't I work cleaning the *fifth*-class cabins, so I could let the poor people enjoy my service?' The manager, of course, accepted my suggestion right away since everyone else wanted to work on the higher-class cabins.

Now my schedule was no longer 9-5, but morning shift and late-night shift of four hours each. When I was on duty, I had to clean the floors of the lounge with broom and mop, scrub the public toilets and shower rooms, and rinse them with a hose. Many of the passengers with fifth class cabin tickets had no beds or seats on which to rest, so they slept and sat in every possible corner of the boat. I wanted to make sure that they knew, by my service and my smile, that they were welcomed [30]. So, whenever and wherever I cleaned, I always made sure that the passenger facilities were as spotless as those of the cruise ship.

I labored diligently and worked up a sweat even when the temperature was under 0°C. This was new to me since my work before was always easy. My parents never let me attempt house work and my hands had never used a broom and mop. My new duties raised hurtful blisters a few days after beginning my new job. When my Mom saw this,

---

[30] Chinese society then seriously discriminated against the peasants.

she asked me whether I wanted my Father to arrange for a new job. I told her not to bother my Father, because I wanted to learn how the other people make a living.

Although I enjoyed making the passengers happy, I did not want to do that job forever. I thought, if I worked hard, my manager would promote me someday. However, this never happened, since he did not seem to like me. He might have disliked me because I looked like a spoiled girl who dressed fashionably and used makeup everyday. Most women still did not use makeup in China then. At the time, I thought I might have to do that job forever, since there was no other option for me.

ARTISTIC INSPIRATION

One day, after I finished washing the public toilets, I returned to the service desk and observed someone lying on the floor. He fell asleep after eating oranges and threw both seeds and shells by his side. I asked myself: 'since this guy appeared to enjoy himself so much, what spirits of freedom and romance gripp him?' He boarded the boat with a standing-room-only ticket, with no reserved bed or seat, so he found a corner in which to lie down. He treated the floor as his bed, fell asleep, and looked most peaceful.

Without shattering the continuity of his peaceful dream, I took white chalk and drew a bed skirt around the place he rested, then, using yellow, drew a small table beside this outline. I surrounded his orange seeds and shells with a plate, and, re-created, alongside, Sichuanese pepper with red chalk. A pair of chopsticks completed this tableau.

I loved my artistic work product and wanted someone to share it, but there was no colleague in sight. In another corner, an old man sat close to my working table. To break the ice, I said 'hi' to him and asked him what he was doing to make a living. He told me he was a fortune teller. Only then, did I realize he was blind.

I thought it might be fun if he would predict my future. I particularly wanted to know my romantic potential with Celebrating China, and the next step in my career. He had me select three cards from a deck and groped for my right hand. He then told me that I would have nothing to do with the man in my mind, that no matter how hard I tried, nothing could come of this fantasy.

I resisted this idea, because I believed if I let Celebrating China know my true feelings, he might end up marrying me. Then, the fortune teller revealed I would soon encounter VIPs to open my world, with great riches in store. He also saw my future career as out distancing my colleagues.

I refused to believe this, and confessed my hope to marry a special man. I protested that my current vocation of cleaning public toilets seemed inconsistent with his glorious predictions. I made him touch the water nozzle used to clean the toilets, and the blisters on my right hand. He instructed me to calm down, cautioned patience, and to wait and see whether he was right.

I did not like what he told me, especially about Celebrating China. So when he asked me to give him 20 cents, I gave him 10 cents. Later, when everything he predicted became true, I regretted my stinginess, but could never find him again to reward him. I did not end up with Celebrating

China no matter how hard I tried. Out of the blue, right at the end of that sailing trip, I was given an interesting and rewarding position.

I AM RESTORED TO LUXURY CRUISING

When my boat reached the dock in Chongqing, I saw a tall beautiful woman in a cruise ship high ranked uniform standing on the deck. She was the manager of the service department on M.S. Ba Shan. Her name was Corinne. I was surprised and could not know why she was there. She waved to me and told me that she was taking me to work on her boat. I told her that it was impossible, because I had to clean the assigned cabins of my current job. In addition, my father promised the HR manager that I would not move around anymore. I believed that my father's promise should be kept.

Corinne told me that she knew how to deal with the HR managers of the passenger boat department and the shipping company. The former was her old friend and the latter was her brother-in-law. She had to get a first permission for me to leave the passenger boat and a second permission for me to work on the cruise line again. Otherwise, my file could not be transferred. During those days, no file meant no identity. Corinne did not let me clean my assigned cabins and we just left, concerned that the HR office would be closed if we did not hurry. I did not return to my cabin to pick up my belongings and left the boat forever.

So, I was given the position of the manager of the Gift Shop & Art Gallery on M.S. Ba Shan. When the accountant read my first financial report, he was amazed how I could do it on my own without any training. He didn't know that I worked as a cashier in a department store of a hotel in downtown Chongqing for six months, immediately after I graduated from high school. Over there, I was given two-months training in bookkeeping. The accountant told me that my job was similar to that of a small business owner, who not only handled inventory and sales but also accounting and bookkeeping tasks. This job also involved handling all of the supply orders and warehouse management for the service department. I enjoyed this new job. The leaders in the higher executive team of the cruise line suggested the shop managers from the other boats visit my shop to learn how it should be done.

When I returned to the luxury environment and compared it to my life on the passenger boat, I felt lucky that I had such a Father, though he had not done anything to advance me this time. I knew I could not have returned to this ship without his reputation playing some role. I also realized how hard it was for an ordinary employee to ascend the career ladder. This time, I cherished my job more, worked hard, and made a lot of money for a 21-year-old girl.

I no longer heard from Celebrating China, learned from someone that he quit his job at the shipping company, and became a business man. I thought I would never see Celebrating China again, because there was no link between his life and mine. However, the year of 2011 was full of surprises. While I was visiting my parents in Chongqing during the summer break, Celebrating China called and told me that he had been looking for me for the past 25 years. I asked how he found my phone number. He said that he was at the office which administraters compensation for the retired executives of the shipping company, and the office staff gave him my Father's phone number. It was shocking to me that he took the effort to find me after 25 years.

Today, I am thankful for Celebrating China's persistent rejection, because it made it possible for me to have such a colorful life rambling around the world. I cannot imagine a wild woman like myself anchored to one place for a whole life. I did regret I couldnot attend college when I was working on the boats. Later I realized that the years of working on the ships provided me more valuable education than any Chinese college, then, could possibly provide. The professors knew very little about the world due to the isolation of China, but many of our passengers were highly educated and informed successful Americans or Chinese leaders. Besides, it was so much more fun to work on ships than to study in a college which could have confined me to one intellectual box.

Singing for International Macroeconomics Forum, 1985

My Last Singing on M.S. Bashan in 1988

DEVELOPMENT ON DRY LAND

MY PARENTS VISION OF A 'NORMAL' LIFE

My rich, materialistic life on the cruise ship upset my parents. They wanted me to live a normal life like anybody else around them. So they requested me to switch to a job on shore. I did not know what that meant, and agreed.

In January 1989, with a recommendation from my Father to the leader of the unit, I went to work as a vehichle examiner in the Computer Control Center for what would be called in the states a 'Department of Motor Vehicles'. Before I started working there, I presumed this job might be technical and challenging, but the reality was the opposite. It was not challenging at all, since it was 100% automated. I felt this was too boring and wastful of my youth, because I had become used to dealing with exotic and interesting human beings. Now I had to face a bunch of machines in a glass-cubicled jail, alone, six days per week.

So the most interesting time for me became technically training students from different cities. I trained several groups of students from Chongqing, Shanghai, Chengdu and other cities that had purchased the same 'DMV' computer systems from Japan. After work, I showed the trainees around the city and had some fun. As usual, after each training was done, new friendships formed.

In March, a group of Chengdu trainees came to our unit for three weeks. They were stationed at the hotel of the college opposite our unit, and came for training classes during weekdays. I found them all humorous and friendly. For some reason, they all called me 'Master One', and liked to be around me.

Our unit had routine security duty turns. Each employee had to take a turn manning the office over weekends. During my turn on duty, the leading trainee, Virtuous, came to wash his Toyota van in our parking lot. My boss, Mr. Feng, saw him and invited him to have dinner with us, so we got to know each other better after the dinner.

After I was off duty, Virtuous invited me to meet his friend, Buddha, who was a business owner and a former executive for the Chongqing Hotel. Since I always enjoyed meeting new people, I gladly accepted the invitation. I went to the dinner at Chongqing Hotel, met Virtuous's friend Buddha and he introduced several of his old colleagues to us.

I enjoyed the dinner and realized that the people who were working for the hotel shared something with which I was familiar: the hospitality business, rather than the operrational rat race of a motor vehicle department. They had gentlemanly manners, in contrasted to the dirty talking, Spartan style behavior of arrogant and corrupted bureaucrats.

After dinner, Virtuous asked me to play Karaoke and I sang the song, *Take Me Home, Country Road,* from the bittersweet memories of the cruise ship. When the bill came, I insisted on paying, he fought with me over this. I told him not to worry, I had the money, because I worked on an American chartered cruise ship, which meant I enjoyed savings that ordinary young people did not have.

When he drove me home, he told me he was impressed with my English and asked why I would stay in such a boring place as Chongqing, instead of studying abroad. The absence of a higher education still hurt. When I recalled the intellectual conversation of the executives at the Chongqing Hotel, I realized studying abroad should be my next immediate goal. Later that year, I enrolled in a night school to improve my English and prepare for the TOEFL test.

THE TIAN AN MEN SQUARE MASSACRE

Not long after the Chengdu training group departed, about April 20th, college students in Beijing started daily peaceful protests. Thus, were sown the seeds of the infamous Tian An Men Square butchery, of which most Westerners have heard. The students requested the government to clean up corruption and implement democratic administration of the bureaucracies.

Soon, college students in Chongqing, in solidarity, occupied our town plaza. I saw buses and trucks containing fired up young students waving and shouting slogans. They, too, demanded democratic reform, especially freedom of speech. For the first time since Mao's Cultural Revolution, people who supported the movement took to the streets.

China Central TV (CCTV) aired the student movement in Tian An Men Square, live, every day, but the central government delayed discussions with the student leaders. In response to the government's lethargy, the students in Tian An Men Square started a hunger strike on May 13th which lasted for a week and spread all over China.

One evening, my classmate Red and I visited downtown Chongqing to see what was up. We saw the students camped in the plaza outside the government buildings, and a big speaker blared updated news from Voice of America (VOA). I questioned the student's choice of Voice of America. They responded that Chinese media, controlled by the government, was not to be trusted, VOA was the only beam of light of truth and freedom. This was the first time I was suggested to doubt the Chinese media.

By May 19th, CCTV reported that the General Party Secretary, Zhao Zi Yang, went to see the hunger striking students in Tian An Men Square and apologized to them for responding too late. While we thought that this might be a turning point, the day after his visit, 180,000 solders armed with machine guns and tanks were sent to Tian An Men Square.

Due to an educational system that never allowed us to doubt the government, I trusted our media 100% and thought the CCTV was doing a great job documenting the progress of the student movement. The image of Wu Er Kai Xi, one of the student leaders, negotiating with Premier Li Peng, and the image of General Party Secretary Zhao Zi Yang apologizing to the protesters, totally convinced me that we had hope of moving toward democracy. I could not understand why the troops were sent there.

To find the truth, Red and I found the Voice of America channel on my parents' radio and listened to it. When my parents saw us glued to the radio, they said nothing, but warned us to be careful when going out. People were distracted from their work and followed the news of the protests daily.

Then I was introduced to a local doctor, Firm Book, as a potential boyfriend. He told me he was required to inject glucose into the veins of hunger striking students in the plaza. He revealed that many of the students just pretended to be striking, but he injected glucose in them as well. He left me a bottle of vitamins and told me that this was imported from America for high officials *only*!

The student movement continued peacefully. Red and I still listened to Voice of America at my parents' home nightly. We thought the students might achieve their goal since the government seemed about to agree to settle with them.

However, our expectations were dashed. One night, my Father returned from work and saw us still listening to Voice of America. He warned us to be careful, since this student movement was not as simple as we thought, and was partially inspired by foreign instigation. He said that the government called him into a meeting, where he was told the student movement was simply being exploited by foreign interests.

The morning after my Father's warning, June 4th, 1989, the troops 'cleaned up' Tian An Men Square and hundreds of students were killed. I was surprised and upset about this outcome. We could not believe what had happened.

My favorite CCTV news reporter, Constitution, appeared on the evening news dressed in black, mourning the students who lost their precious lives. She reported that the central government defined this student movement as 'anti-revolutionary violence'. The news said that violent agitators mixing with the students upset the previous peaceful protests and promoted the bloodshed. Many soldiers were attacked, and some killed. The armed forces had intervened to stop the chaos, it was reported.

My Father bought into this story right away. Mom suspected the opposite. I was totally confused and did not know what to believe.

Then suddenly, my favorite news reporter, Constitution, disappeared from CCTV. I never saw her again on the air. Presumably she was dismissed for showing sympathy to the dead students by wearing black while reporting the news on June 4th, 1989.

Soon, General Xu Qin Xian was sentenced to jail for five years, due to his rejection of Deng Xiao Ping's direct order to invading Tian An Men Square[31]. Top intellectuals like Yan Jia Qi, who supported General Party Secretary Zhao Zi Yang's political reform, were now listed as traitors and wanted by the government. They escaped to France during the chaos, along with Zhao Zi Yang's children and other movement leaders. Zhao Zi Yang himself was placed under house arrest and remained so until the end of his life in 2005.

BRAINWASHING BLOOD STAINS

Thereafter, at work, we began to receive documents from the central government about a new campaign to 'clean up corruption', every morning. We were required to write reports about where we had been and who we were with during the past two months. Although most people had

---

[31] I couldn't understand why Deng Xiao Ping made that order then, but now I think I might have an answer. This movement might have reminded Deng Xiao Ping what happened during the chaotic Cultural Revolution time. He might have regretted that Liu Shao Qi didn't forcefully stop the Red Guards at the beginning of the Cultural Revolution.

supported or joined this movement, now we were forced to lie to protect ourselves.

As a result of this political reeducation, I changed my anti-dictator stance to pro-dictator. Some student leaders of this movement also changed their position when they experienced, later, rapid economic growth. Most people cannot resist injected ideas, while minority views are repressed. I was not an exception.

Brainwashing may change common sense and make us feel that the *imposed* doctrine arises from our hearts. We would refuse to accept the truth of our brainwashing, even when someone demonstrated it with bloody evidence. It is the same everywhere, including in today's Western societies.

This is the mechanism by which the Chinese society forgot the 36 million plus deaths caused by starvation after the Great Leap Forward movement; this is how we forgot our best teachers had spent their most valuable youth in jails, or communing with cows; this is how we forgot the truth of the Tian An Men massacre. However, we never forgot the Opium War, nor the Nanking Massacre. We only remember the propaganda we were fed.

LOVE IN A PRISON

RESCUING VIRTUOUS FROM HIS VICE

In September 1989, my colleague brought me a copy of the Sichuan Daily. This was the provincial newspaper. It reported that Chengdu's Procuratorate had arrested some corrupted policemen for taking bribes.

One of them was Virtuous, the individual who was one of my trainees. We had gotten along well. We felt so sorry for Virtuous, because corruption was, to us, no big deal - business as usual. So we did not see him as terribly evil, and had sympathy for him.

Then, I received a long letter from Virtuous' father. He begged me to help his son, because he had threatened suicide while imprisoned. Even though he was isolated in jail, his father had asked him whom he knew might be of help; he told his father that I might be that person.

I am someone who embraces challenges and likes to help people, so I wrote back to Virtuous' father and told him that I would try my best to help. I thought Virtuous might have made the occasional mistake, but had a good heart. So on one weekend, when Virtuous's father asked me to meet him in Cheng Du, I met him and other Virtuous' family members.

However, I didn't agree with his father's view that the people who reported his son's misconduct were to blame. I acknowledged that in every human life there could be some mistakes, I emphasized that should Virtuous be rescued, he should cease making similar mistakes. His family supported this view.

After this meeting, I wrote a letter to Virtuous to express my concerns and offered my help. He was grateful. Then, like all imprisoned creatures, he became more and more emotionally dependent upon me.

In the spring of 1990, he was sentenced to jail for 20 years. Virtuous threatened, again, to kill himself. I comforted him, begged him not to take his own life, and assured we would obtain his release. His parents and I continued working with lawyers and friends. After a great initial effort, we had his sentence reduced to 10 years. Then we were told there were 'alternative' means to reduce his sentence other than through the court system. We learned that Virtuous took bribes worth 40,000 yuan, which was about the equivalent of $5,000 USD then. Though a substantial offense, a 10-year sentence still sounded excessive to me.

To abate the chances of his suicide, I promised his parents that I would write him every week, and visit him as often as I could. So, with the assistance from a friend, Virtuous was transferred to a jail in Cheng Du, Sichuan province, which had a printing facility with inmate workers.

It was about 30 minutes' distance by car from his home in the center of Chengdu. However, I had to take an over night train to visit him from Chongqing.

AN ILLICIT LOVE

For the first three months after the trial, I visited him in jail once a month but wrote him every week. Maybe the time and energy devoted to comfort him was too much, too soon. Meeting his emotional needs became a habit, and I could not develop relationships with other young men. So, when he told me that his wife would never return to him and punched his head on the wall, I consoled him that he still had me.

Thereafter, our letters became intimate, and I began visiting him every week. Every Saturday evening, I got on the 9:59 pm train from Chongqing and arrived Chengdu at 7:59 am on Sunday morning. I typically visited his parents and his son Coco first, then brought him a shared lunch prepared by his parents.

After lunch, I would take Coco to have some fun in the Children's Palace, helped him with his homework until I had to catch the 9:59 pm train back to Chongqing. Poor little Coco had no parenting for over a year, and became more and more attached to me. He kissed me whenever he got a chance. He clung to me whenever I had to leave for Chongqing.

Sometimes, I was too late to purchase either a sleeper or seat on the train to Chongqing. I had to do laps around the train during the trip and went to work directly from the train station. My parents noticed changes in my health and became very worried about me. They knew that if they tried to stop me, it would only spur me on. So all they could do was just waiting for me to come to my senses.

I commuted to the jail weekly for a year and a half. His jailers were touched and became my friends. They even let Virtuous have his own proofreading office, and we cooked dumplings in an improvised kitchen. Incredibly, I lost my virginity in that jail office. I just felt compelled to submit to his sexual overtures or he might self-destruct. There was no joy in this physical intimacy to me.

Virtuous said that he would return my wonderful grace with 10,000 folds of love once released. It is hard to express how I felt about this intimacy, because my body was not mature enough to know what to expect. The whole experience was rather a negative one.

So, his parents and I worked even harder to obtain his release. We consulted powerful friends. They suggested to use health issues as leverage. So Virtuous had a comprehensive checkup with the jail doctor. The doctor's report said that though all organs were healthy, his neck had a problem. Using this flimsy medical excuse, he was released eight years earlier than he should have been. Of course, the process was not that simple, and entailed lots of help from friends. As is the case with everything else, the costs could not be measured by money alone.

In the fall of 1991, Virtuous's father told me that his release would occur before the year end. I was delighted, but concerned about the nature of our relationship, because he was still legally married. Though attached to him, I did not want myself to be the reason of his divorce.

So I took a year off and enrolled in an English program at Sichuan Foreign Studies Institution preparing to pursue my higher education abroad. I did not want to date anybody, although suitors were not in short supply.

Virtuous got out of jail in mid-December of 1991. I did not meet him at the gate of the jail. He did not repay my wonderful grace with 10,000 folds of love, as he had earlier promised.

Instead, he fell in love with a beautiful musician, Gorgeous. Of course, *he* didn't tell me - Gorgeous, a cello player, told on him. She was born in the year of the tiger, 5 years my elder.

Gorgeous's revelation reminded me of Virtuous's complaint that I behaved, in bed, like a piece of wood. I thought, perhaps, I had some fault in his betrayal. So, when Virtuous came to Chongqing to apologize for his infidelity, I decided to give our relationship another chance.

DANCING WITH WOLVES

THE NINE DRAGON SEAFOOD RESTAURANT

In early 1992, Virtuous visited Chongqing, I never mentioned the cello player Gorgeous or accused him. I focused on what we should do for the future. We first decided that he could run a restaurant because he loved food and cooking. We chose to implement a high-end Cantonese-style seafood restaurant, because such cuisine generated substantial profit.

By this time, the economic reform had continued for 6 years; most of the economy was still government owned. The government had been gradually deregulating, encouraging people who had entrepreneurial spirit to lease some government owned businesses or properties. Thus, we had a great opportunity to enter the market.

My high school classmates, Jimmy, located the president of Chongqing Cuisine Service Company, which owned all the restaurants in Chongqing. We requested permission to lease a restaurant that had large square footage. The president thought this a great idea, since none of the government owned restaurants were profitable. He suggested the largest restaurant space available in downtown, just across the street from Chongqing Guest House, a four-star hotel.

It was a Muslim restaurant[32], and we had to abide by the rules of Muslim culture. We could not sell ugly animals, such as fish with no scales and fins, or yellow eels and crabs. In addition, this was a pork-free restaurant.

The president told us that it was government policy to locate Muslim restaurants in every district in China for the convenience of traveling Muslims, and pinpoint their locations on every map. If we broke their rules, it may cause serious political chaos - so we had to be careful when participating in economic reform.

We thought this acceptable, since we wanted to run a seafood restaurant; not selling pork or ugly animals was fine. That is not to suggest that shrimps were matinee idols. Of most importance was the location, which was prime. In addition, the president agreed to retire the current employees at low cost, and the lease fee was minimal.

Virtuous was satisfied with the prospect of a Muslim restaurant, and signed the lease agreement. However, he did not have a dime to refurnish this large restaurant, its lobby, and eight VIP rooms. New kitchen equipment for Cantonese style cooking required a lot of capital. So, I gave him all my savings from the years of working on the cruise ship and borrowed personal savings from my parents, brothers and relatives.

The total cost for the restuarant reached one million yuan, and the amount we raised was not enough; I borrowed more money from companies in which my relatives had an interest. Then, we borrowed the rest from a bank. All my

---

[32] Residual, Mao-inspired 'equality' called for making the cuisine of diverse cultural entities available throughout China.

friends tried their best to help based on my family's reputation. I believed that Virtuous would cherish the chance of a vocational rebirth.

We spent three months purchasing supplies and refurnishing the restaurant. The result was the most beautiful and largest private restaurant in town at that time. Its main dinning room was on the second floor. Live fish swam in different fish tanks along the wall on the right side, a huge colorful shell hung on the front wall, to the left were four VIP rooms and an office, on either side of the entrance were the cashier and the bar. There were four more bigger VIP rooms on the first floor, along with the kitchen. The exterior wall and the front door were decorated with 'new tech' computerized neon lights that change patterns automatically: big jumping fish and blue ocean waves moved in synchronicity.

We recruited my high school classmate, Jimmy, as vice president and recruited Cantonese chefs from Guangzhou. We also hired handsome young boys and beautiful girls as servers.

The sailor's orchestra from my Father's company played music in their white uniforms for a magnificent opening of the Nine Dragon Seafood Restaurant.

The Chongqing TV station reported the opening to the whole city. Hundreds of our guests from all sectors attended this celebration, enjoyed our food, and complimented the services and uniforms of our service employees. It was quite a busy and exciting evening for all of us.

The following four weeks of operation were great, with over two thousand dollars's worth of revenue each day. If we kept this pace, we could pay back all the loans in one year.

However, things did not turn out the way I expected.

A MIDNIGHT VISITOR

One night when I was sleeping, someone knocked at the door. It was almost midnight. I could not imagine who it might be. I got up and opened the door. It was an elegant woman. I suddenly realized the visitor must be Virtuous's wife, because I had seen her pictures with her son Coco.

After she entered and sat down, I was informed that she had come to claim her legal status as Virtuous' wife, since they were not going to divorce. I told her that I heard a completely different story from Virtuous and his parents, and didn't want to interfere with their marriage.

After she left, I wondered, 'how the hell did she discover my address'? From Virtuous? Likely, but why would he do that? I could not understand.

After a sleepless night, I went to work and found out that Virtuous's wife had also called my boss at the DMV. She told him that I was having an affair with her husband, and requested him to criticize me. Utterly embarrassed, I wanted to find Virtuous and force an explanation. So, I went to the restaurant.

When Virtuous saw the expression of my face, he asked me to have a cup of coffee at the Chongqing Guest House, opposite our restaurant. Believing he did not want our staff members as audience, I followed him. At the coffee bar, I asked him whether he had taken his wife to my home. He didn't reply.

I informed him we were done as lovers, but we needed to rationally sort out the financial details of the business, in order to protect the investments from my relatives and family members. He agreed. Then we walked back to the restaurant.

YET ANOTHER TIGER WOMAN BARES HER CLAWS

Before re-entering, our bookkeeper Dawn walked toward me and asked to speak with me.
Dawn: "Are you still Virtuous' girlfriend?"
Me: "Yes, why do you ask?"
Dawn: "He told me you broke up. We slept together. I do not believe him. I think he cares about you more than he cares about me."
Then, she showed me two bottles of sleeping pills.
Dawn: "I am going to make Virtuous take them, if he does not, then I would take them all."
She looked desperate, drawn.
Dawn: "I requested Virtuous prevent you from entering the restaurant. He promised he would."
Dawn reminded me of the cello player, Gorgeous[33]. They both were exceptionally beautiful, with big breasts. Dawn was 19 years old, 12 years younger than Gorgeous. They both were born in the years of tiger. Looking at her, I realized that all tiger women I encountered were extremely beautiful. My Mom was one of them.
Me: "Now I am done with him. He is all yours."
I now realized Virtuous was just a user. His repetitive conducts proved he was rotten to the core. What the hell was

---

[33] Gorgeous was Virtuous's first love affair after he got out of jail.

going on with his wife? My heart was broken again, but I had little time for self-pity. I had to protect the funds I borrowed from everyone and everywhere. Both equity and liabilities were under his name, since the rest of us were working for the government, and not allowed to own businesses.

I told Dawn that Virtuous had not invested a dime in this restaurant, but my family had. Then she confessed Virtuous had not deposited revenues in the bank. Instead, he stole all the cash from the safe daily, and no one knew where the money had gone. I never considered such a possibility. Dawn let the cat out of the bag.

THE WOLVES EMERGE

Dawn and I angrily charged into the main dinning room. I saw a group of regular customers sitting there. One of them was Crimson, a police captain of the vice squad. We said hello to each other. Then I chased Virtuous into the kitchen because he was trying to avoid me. I asked him to come out from hiding place, so we could speak.

He agreed and followed Dawn and I to the outside. Before we got far, Crimson and his team suddenly appeared in front of us, arrested Virtuous, and hand cuffed him. Dawn and I were shocked, then realized that there must be more to this story. So, we followed them to the police office.

Once there, Crimson ordered Virtuous onto the floor and kicked his rear end, while vowing 'to pound this piece of shit from Chongqing back to Chengdu'. Crimson could not understand why this 38-year-old scoundrel, who was not handsome, had no money, was married infidel, and had a loyal young girlfriend, could charm the 19-year-old sexually awakening Dawn to fall for him head over heal. I was totally confused about this rapidly disintegrating situation. Facts, falsehoods, infamy, innuendos, betrayals, and financial ruin rocketed around in my brain like pachinko balls, and gave me a blinding headache. I felt miserable and had no inclination to face friends or family.

I was so embarrassed I wanted to leave Chongqing forever, but I still wondered whether Virtuous had ever loved me, or just used me. I wanted to discover this, and called the police captain Crimson, the next day. He invited me to have hotpot with his teammates. So, I went.

During this meal, Crimson told me, during Virtuous captivity, he asked him which girl he loved the most. Virtuous claimed I was his true love, and that Dawn was just a plaything. He also informed me the real reason for Virtuous' arrest.

Virtuous borrowed 60,000 Yuan (close to $8,000 USD's worth) from Winter (a drug dealer previously unknow to me) and had not paid it back. Later I found out that Winter was a close friend of Crimson. In China, it was normal for the police to outcompete criminals in the commission of crime.

Of course, Crimson initially claimed that Winter was just a friend, but the luxury mink coat Crimson sported was obvious evidence of corruption. Such a garment on a California Highway Patrolman might raise some eyebrows. Such a coat would have cost Crimson two years of honest income in 1992. He boasted he was the great economic success of his family.

Crimson's wife, Ali, was the older sister of my best girlfriend in highschool class, the School Flower. The four of us used to play card games together at Ali's home. Later, although Crimson knew his wife was close to me, he still asked Dawn for a date in my presence.

Crimson told me that Virtuous did not repay the money he owed to Winter on time, as he promised. He could not understand, he said, how the money disappeared. He believed it was impossible for Virtuous to spend as much money as he had stolen in such a short period of time, even if he eaten money and defecated it.

CONFRONTING THE WOLVES

I did not have a clue where the money had gone, either. However, I knew that throwing him in jail would neither be good for the business nor help return of the money. So, I asked Crimson to release Virtuous to run the restaurant. He refused.

I then threatened him, "If you do not let Virtuous out in 24 hours, I will report you to the People's Delegation of Chongqing Municipality that you are implicated in the illegal loan business of a known drug dealer."

When Crimson heard this threat, he exclaimed: "Hey, you are not as simple as I thought. How come I never realized that?"

So, Crimson gave me daily custoday of Virtuous for restaurant operations, but he had him monitored by cops until he was safely back in a cell each evening. When I asked Virtuous why he was arrested, he said he borrowed money from the drug dealer Winter, and when Winter saw the restaurant was doing well he wanted to own it. Winter tried to force Virtuous to sell the restaurant below cost to him.

Virtuous told Winter he could not, so he had Crimson arrested him.

I contrived to let Virtuous escape Chongqing by smuggling him aboard a boat bound for Shanghai. My purpose was to obtain answers to 'my one million questions.' Virtuous and I travelled all the way to Shanghai, but returned on the same boat within two weeks. During the trip, we had deep conversations that echo in my mind to this day. Virtuous regretted all the bad things he did. He was contrite and apologized. However, this did not heal the wounds in my heart.

Upon our return to Chongqing, its street life reminded me of everything negative. Virtuous still would not explain to me where the money had gone. I resented his repeated betrayals and deposited him at Crimson's office. This was my first time to intentionally wound someone who trusted me. My previous forgiveness inspired his trust. This time, I promised myself, I would harden my heart - and not relent - no matter how he begged me.

DIVING INTO THE SEA OF COMMERCE

THE APPRENTICE

At the time I decided to leave Virtuous in the tender mercies of the police, I also decided to leave him - and Chongqing forever.

I asked a friend for a recommendation letter to obtain a job in Guangzhou. Then I called my boss and requested one year off. He understood my situation and granted leave.

In Guangzhou, my recommendation letter earned me an interview dinner with a Hong Kong executive, Honor. Honor believed that I could be an assistant to the president of his firm, Menpo Engineering, which designed and produced commercial kitchen equipment for high end hotels. I did not know whether I could do it, but would try my best. I would begin immediately.

During the dinner, I told Honor my pathetic restaurant story, and asked him to find potential buyer for me. He said he would research the matter and see what he might help. I determined to try every possibility to sell the restaurant.

The next morning, Honor took me to his factory in Fongchun district. I met the staff and toured the plant. All of them spoke Cantonese which I could not understand. After lunch, I met one of their clients.

Dinner was arranged at a large restaurant owned by the Army, with multiple floors containing fancy VIP rooms armed with Karaoke systems. They had such a good business their next expansion was twice the size. After being introduced to the manager of the restaurant, my new employer assigned me the task of delivering architectural plans to clients from time to time.

I was also introduced to various key bureaucrats, including Chief of the Environment Bureau of Guangdong Province. I worked hard and learned fast, paid no attention to anything else but my work.

About a month later, I was assigned to travel to Chongqing with my boss Honor in pursuit of a new project. This excited me, because Honor would have the chance to introduce my restaurant operation - hopefully - to potential buyers. So I called my Mom and told her that I was coming home. Mom told me that Virtuous sent her a letter informing her that he was in jail again, and begged her to send him a quilt.

Chongqing was extremely cold and humid in December. I could not imagine how to survive there for a single night without a quilt. My Mom did not understand why Virtuous was in jail again, but she pitied him and brought a quilt to the jail. Surprisingly, when she asked to visit Virtuous, the jail police told her that there was no such person by that name in custody. After showing them his letter, the jail police accepted the quilt but did not let her see Virtuous. Later, my second brother Banyan told me that he learned Virtuous had been booked under the name of a suspected murderer. This worried me.

VIRTUOUS, IMPRISONED BY WOLVES

When I arrived in Chongqing, I called captain Crimson, and asked him where I might find Virtuous. He admitted he was with Winter. I told him the need to locate Virtuous, because he was the only person who had the legal right to convey title to the restaurant.

He revealed that Winter and Virtuous were in the Chongqing Guest House.

I found Winter's room number from the front desk and went there. When I rang the bell, a young man opened the door. As I walked through, I saw two young men injecting each other in the bedroom. This was the first time I encountered the use of hard drugs, and did not then know how heroine was administered. I thought they were sick and did not want to go to a hospital.

I told these characters they should not be doing this themselves, and suggested them to seek medical professionals. They did not respond to me, so I walked into the sitting room where Virtuous and Winter were watching TV. I told Winter I was taking Virtuous to meet a potential buyer for the restaurant, and he did not stop me. But he barked an order at the drug addicts, "Follow them!"

Virtuous, Honor and I had dinner at the Jade Restaurant in the Chongqing Hotel. We discussed the potential sale of the restaurant while enjoying our meal. Then one of the two drug addicts tapped Virtuous on the shoulder and asked him to leave the table.

Virtuous left with the addict. In a few minutes, a security guard came in and informed us that two men were beating up our guest at the gate of the hotel. When we went out, Virtuous was being sequentially kicked on the back and stomach by the two drug addicts - back and forth like a football - but he did not strike back. I insisted the addicts cease beating him, they stopped and took him away.

VIRTUOUS ESCAPES THE WOLVES LAIR

Since I was worried that they might kill Virtuous, I asked my two brothers to help. We decided to get Virtuous out of Chongqing and let my brother History run the restaurant and assisted by my classmate Jimmy. I rang the bell once more, and the door was opened by one of the two addicts.

Winter was watching TV. I informed him that Virtuous had to negotiate with my potential buyer, and we took him away again. Since Winter did not ask the two addicts to follow this time, I wondered why. We took Virtuous to my brother History's home, and he signed an authorization letter for History to be able to sell the restaurant.

The next day, Virtuous and I flew to Guangzhou with my boss Honor. In Guangzhou, Virtuous had to stay with me, for he had no money. I told him to try to find a job. He tried. He had no luck.

My work schedule became more and more busy. Virtuous complained that I worked too hard for too little income, and he barely saw me. He suggested I ask my boss Honor for a commission plus salary. Honor agreed, promised 5% commission for each commercial kitchen project I secured.

During the Spring Festival, most migrant city workers returned to the countryside for the long holiday. Virtuous and I decided to go to Shenyang, Liao Ning province, to visit his older sister's family. Shen Yang is in northeast of China, and very cold in winter. I had never seen a snow-covered city before then.

I borrowed some money from my employer, told them that I would go to Shenyang for the holidays, but would also check out potential clients there. President Yang told me if I found prospective clients, I did not have to return, but stay there and seal any deal. The office would wire me expenses as requested.

MY FIRST EXPLORATION IN NORTHERN CHINA

We landed in Shenyang before Spring Festival Eve. On the way to Virtuous' sister Bell's home, I saw a forest of chimneys, and piles of black stuff along both sides of the roads. The temperature of this place was -11°F; I assumed the weather was cold enough that people had to pile coal near the buildings to secure immediate supply. However, the piles were not coal, but snow covered with ashes.

The family gathering was pleasant. Virtuous' elder sister Bell and her family members were wonderful, loving, caring and generous people. They took us to dinner parties with many of their friends, colleagues and family members, every night during our visit.

Bell and her husband, Culture, had one daughter Rose, a sweet and diligent high school student. Culture was the president of a government owned entity in the fire extinguishing system business. They all knew that Virtuous had gone to prison, but still welcomed us as their respected guests.

Virtuous asked Culture what business they might do together. Culture responded that he would rather do business with me instead. Obviously, he had no confidence in Virtuous, although he still cared about his well being.

After the Spring Festival of 1993, Culture's sales manager brought me to a project cite in Shenyang, Gloria Plaza, then under construction. This project was developed by the army. The president and the chairman of the board was Commander Huang. His father was the first party secretary of Liaoning province, and participated in the famous Red Army's Long March with Chairman Mao. This is a big deal in China.

When welcomed by commander Huang at his office, I noticed it was large enough to make a visitor feel extremely small and unimportant.

Commander Huang thanked me for coming from so far to represent our company and its products. This warm welcome of guests from remote locations had to do with the fact that travel had been restricted in China since 1949. Until 1993, People could not travel far without national ration tickets for food. By the Chinese way of thinking, I was, to them, more of a precious guest than a potential supplier.

After that first meeting, I invited Commander Huang to have lunch at the Hong Kong Gourmet Restaurant in town. Of course, he came with a coterie of attendants. I knew we had became true friends after this lunch, because from then on, he insisted on dining at more modest restaurants.

To reciprocate the friendship from Commander Huang, Culture, and his family, I made Sichuan Style pork sausages from scratch. I had my Father send me the casings, and bought spices obtained from the local market. I made ten kilograms of Sichuan Sausage without following a recipe. I did not have a chance to taste them before they were given away. Fortunately, all the recipients responded with high compliments.

Commander Huang told me that his family had received several kinds of sausages as gifts for the Spring Festival. His mother told him that the dark colored sausages, made by me, tasted the best of all.

I was so proud of my first achievement as a cook. I had never prepared anything except fast noodles. Now, the confidence found in making sausages made me believe that I could do anything I wanted.

Since the sausages were such a hit, our business relationship developed smoothly. We had only two competitors, one smaller than our company, the other the industry leader. Competition with the industry leader was hard since it had much superior resources, but their prices were much higher than ours. That company's interaction with the Commander was not as close as ours although was introduced by a friend of the Commander's son. So, even before the commander raised the money to finish the project, I believe he made up his mind that he would do business with me once he raised the fund.

Then, I was introduced to another project in Dalian by a different colleague of Culture. This project was owned by the Dalian Branch of China Construction Bank. I visited the project office and introduced myself to the Purchasing

Manager, Li. He told me that I was too late, since they had already decided to give the project to the industry leader to build. I offered to make a presentation for future considerations, he agreed.

I guess he gave his consent because it was hard for him to reject someone who had traveled from so far away. After my presentation, I gave him my business card and told him that I was staying at the hotel nearby, and would welcome further inquiry about our company at any time.

Intuition told me to tarry in Dalian, I decided to enjoy its fresh seafood and beautiful scenery, while searching for new business. The weather was beautiful, with gorgeous blue skies, and an ocean of the same color. The bright sun showered me with its rays, bestowed a glowing golden halo on the red fox cape I wore that day.

While I was walking into a restaurant for lunch, a middle-aged woman patted me on my shoulder.

She said to me, "You must pick three cards from the deck, because I saw a golden ring about you as you walked into the restaurant. You must have great fortune ahead." I knew it was probably a fortuneteller's trick to make money, but still took three cards for fun.

She said, "The three cards told me that you will meet a powerful person this year; a flood of money is coming to your way, and you will have a healthy and happy family life."

I did not believe her because I had just rejected by a major potential client. Who would introduce me to such a powerful figure as she prophesied? However, in exchange for her good wishes, I still gave her five Yuan and left.

She restated, "All that is predicted will come true whether you believe me or not."

After lunch, I toured the beach with Culture's colleagues, then retired to the hotel. After I fell asleep, exhausted in my bed, the phone rang. It was Manager Li. What a surprise! I would have never dreamed that he would call me back. Manager Li invited me for a talk at his office. I met him and his wife there, and I was offered an opportunity to win the contract if we could meet their requirements.

One of their requirements, of course, was to know how much kickback this couple would receive if they gave us the project. I told them this was the province of my boss. The wife said to me, "I like your taste of clothing, let's shop together in Shenzhen."

So, since Shenzhen had lots of beautiful clothings from all over the world, and I liked shopping there too. I called my boss in the morning. He instructed me to invite the couple to visit our factory in Guangzhou and our projects in Shenzhen.

The couple accepted the invitation, we traveled to Guangzhou, visited our office at the Victoria Hotel, and met my boss. I showed them the hotel projects in Guangzhou and Shenzhen, then shopped with his wife.

Manager Li told me that he decided to do business with our company. He also asked to borrow $40,000 HK dollars (worth about $5000 USD then) from my boss, when he and his president traveled to Hong Kong and Singapore a month later. I told him this was possible.

MY FIRST MILLION DOLLAR BABY

My boss Honor agreed to Manager Li's request. After they returned to Dalian, my boss and our team flew to Dalian to sign the contract with the chairman of the board, Mr. Cong. I was so excited having secured, on my own, this first project.

The signing ceremony occurred in downtown Dalian at a formal dinner. My boss Honor was surprised that I brought Virtuous along, after so many awful things had happened.

He told me that I was a stupid melon, but he turned out to be a stupid melon himself, because he was in love with a young Chongqingnese girl, Si Si, who also betrayed him.

Honor understood that we both victims of our own sentimental dreams. We both knew that the rest of the world viewed us as the most stupid melons, but we could not resist the seduction of adventure.

We both would rather work hard to overcome the challenges fallen man and woman had inflicted upon us than to accept an ordinary life - a life free of such exquisite pains.

So we toasted our mutual stupidity, our courage for pursuing the challenges of life in our own eccentric ways. Alcohol can help such toasts seem rational. Then we had another toast celebrating my first one million USD contract. President Cong sang a song for us, and signed the contract.

The next day, Honor flew directly to Macao to gamble with Si Si, and I worked with our engineer Mr. Shi on the project site.

When I returned to Guangzhou office, Honor did not give me the 5% of the 2 million yuan (worth nearly $300k USD then) down payment that my client had paid. Instead, he gave me 5,000 yuan every time I begged him. It upset me, because I could do little with 5,000 yuan. Such paltry payment would not buy me a home and was rapidly consumed by hotel fees. If he paid me 100k yuan at one time, I could use it for a down payment of a condominium in Guangzhou. I fought him for the money I deserved, but he ignored it.

SWITCHING MANGERS

So one of my colleagues, Miss Qiu, believed that since Honor did not treat me fairly, I should change companies. She said she knew an owner of a much bigger company with factories in Singapore, Hong Kong and Shenzhen. She called its owner Mr. Tang, and told him that she had a smart and beautiful girl for him as his new sales manager. She bragged about me a bit, so Mr. Tang apparently was excited to meet me the next day.

The meeting went well; Mr. Tang was amazed that I had achieved so much so quick in an unfamiliar industry. He said he would wait for me to finish my responsibilities at my current company. Also, he took the responsibility for potential retaliation against Ms. Qiu, who introduced me to him. He offered to reimburse her salary every month of unemployment, were she fired for helping me.

Mr. Tang asked me what I expected as salary. I told him that I didn't want to be paid a salary: I would like to be his agent in mainland China, if I could take 20% of the total amount of each booked contract as my commission. He loved this idea, and offered me an apartment at his executives' building in Shenzhen, adding, "Any time you need money, just ask me or president Zhao, and they will wire it as soon as possible."

Later, Honor lost money from his gambling spree in Macao. He then failed to pay me the commission I had earned. So I quit that job in the fall of 1993, and started my new work as PRC representative of the new company.

Before the Spring Festival of 1994, Shen Yang Gloria Plaza received new capital and restarted the construction. I told Commander Huang that I changed companies, but was still in the same business. He expected me to do the project for them. So I signed the contract with commander Huang on behalf of my new company.

Then I called the President Cong of Dalian Jin Yuan Hotel, and asked him how the project was going. He was mad at my former boss Honor, since he shipped only a few units to the project site after receiving the two million yuan down payment. He requested Honor to send more equipment before making his next payment, Honor refused to do this without further payment. I apologized to President Cong, expressed sorrow that I had no control over Honor. So President Cong asked me whether I knew another company which could take over the project, and I informed him of my new position. He then asked me to go to Dalian to finish the work, and I was delighted to do so.

I flew to Dalian and made another contract with President Cong. Before I calculated the offering prices, I asked whether I should include the kick-back like they did with Honor before. He refused to take any kick-back and complained, "the ethics of our cadres is pitiable!"

So, I gave him a big discount and included extra equipment in the price. He promptly accepted and signed the contract with me in his office. He even refused my invitation for a celebratory dinner.

With a Colleague in Our Hong Kong Office,
May 5th, 1995

CELEBRATING SUCCESS

During the first six months at the new company, I made enough money to take care of the problems caused by our failed restaurant. I called History on the phone and asked if he had any luck selling it. He told me that it was sold to someone at a discount. To cure my mistakes, I sent him all the money that we owed to all the relatives and friends. History was surprised that I had been able to make restitution in such a short time.

I also wanted to reward, with cash, Culture's colleagues who had introduced the two new projects to me. Culture warned me not to do it, because they were employees of a government owned company. So, I bought two Nikon cameras from Hong Kong and gave one to each of them as gifts. That satisfied them.

Due to Culture's upright character, I did not dare to mention compensating him. The only thing I did for his family was to buy clothes, shoes and purses for them whenever I travelled back to Hong Kong or Shenzhen. I wanted to buy them a bigger TV set, but they would not accept it. I always felt that I owed them, because what they did for me could not be measured by money. So I tutored their daughter Rose in mathematics before the college entrance test. They were amazed that I still remembered maths so well after having left high school for almost 10 years.

After a stressful year, I decided to take a long holiday enjoying the warm weather in Shenzhen. One day, when I was having lunch with a friend, he showed me a real estate ad in a newspaper, and suggested I buy a condominium in downtown Shenzhen.

We went to the developer's office and I bought a unit with three bedrooms, in a 36-floor high rise. Our company wired the check as payment in full the next day. I was glad that my new company always kept its promises, unlike my former employer.

Then I returned to Chongqing to see my parents. They were happy to see me, and I assured them that I would not cause them further grief. They expressed their love for me and forgave all the mistakes I made in the past. I had a good time with them, and bought them whatever they needed for the house. They tried hard to prevent me buying anything for them. They also requested I quit my DMV job, because they did not want people to conclude their daughter had been fired, so I quit.

HOOKERS ON THE HOOF

My business developed smoothly, and my satisfied clients generated more. As compensation to his family who had done so much for me, I hired Virtuous to coordinate some of the project sites under construction. I did not have to do this, because each project had a Hong Kong manager. I gave him this job to keep him busy, because like a whipped mongrel, he followed me everywhere. This afforded me some privacy and peace. He enjoyed wining and dining our clients, playing karaoke, and hanging out with the "San Pei" - beautiful young girls who can do much more than sing.

'San' means three and 'Pei' means company. So a 'San Pei' girl is like an escort who accompanies a client to eat, drink and sing. Although illegal, the clients - with the girls's consent - could pay to whisk them away for a long evening.

I was shocked when I first saw teenage hookers soliciting clients at a roadside restaurant in the early 90's. I finally became numb to this having seen numerous hookers in the Karaoke night clubs all over China. They were extremely young and beautiful, mostly under 20.

I guess many of them were under the thumb of the mafia which controlled them through drugs. Some who were not on drugs would sing and dance or drink with the men. Those on drugs unceremoniously let the men fondle them.

These women were highly organized and professionally trained with skills, such as, dirty talk, enticing rap, seductive dances, and sexually flirty games. Probably more, since I could not see their private practices.

Dongguan is an industrial town neighboring Shenzhen, famous for its extremely young and beautiful hooker population. My colleague's younger brother once told me that a 19 years old hooker was over the hill. I was speechless when I heard this.

My high school classmate Yu Yan, the successful real estate developer and poet, wrote a verse about the features of Dongguan hookers, which should be shared with the world:

Old Hooker

The smoke of the world of men
cannot provoke a ripple in her heart,
She only longs to make love to an elephant
a strong adult male
two tons in weight
with skin as wrinkled as the Great Wall.
Imagine this fierce scene:
her monstrous flood of blood,
cascading over her perishing vessels,
back and forth.

*O she has handled numerous weapons
sufficient to arm an expeditionary force.
She knows well the distinctive
quality of weapons
from different classes
so well,
she imagines giving guest lectures
in Beijing University or on China Central TV.*

*Her popularity must rise above that of
the old woman
who treated the Analects of Confucius
like costume jewelry.
Her direction of research?
Hair, fingernails, teeth . . .
all the bodily derivatives
and those beyond body -
the fluid glance, the breathless moan, the
facials grimaces and grins . . .
all the non-physical cultural heritage,
those contents that ordinary people ignore
should transcend the altitude of the professionals.*

*She says she is old
like falling leaves returning to their roots,
but she can't remember her hometown,
can't remember the man who plucked her
from the slopes of a mountain village.
She only remembers a small town called Dongguan.
The empty pools of her eyes
seem farther away*

than the Tang Dynasty.
This year, she will turn 20 years of age.
    -By Yu Yan

VIRTUOUS DESCENDS INTO VICE

In the winter of 1994, one of the investors of Shen Yang Gloria Plaza invested in a new project, called Dalian International Exhibition Center. I asked Commander Huang's girlfriend Susan to work for me and take charge of this project, so she could make some money in addition to her teaching job.

Susan was a vice professor in Northeastern Financial Institute. She did a great job for us throughout the tender bidding and the construction processes. I gave her extra commissions, so she could buy her dream home by the beach. She had previously lived in a very small studio provided by her school.

Virtuous was upset that I placed Susan in charge of this project but not him. Sulking, he began to indulge himself.

I so remember the time I flew to Dalian to check on my projects. He met me at the airport - looking ugly.

In the evening, he confessed to me that he made a mistake.

"What mistake? Another woman, AGAIN?"

"In order to avoid making the woman mistake again, I made a different kind of mistake."

I could not imagine what that could be. I did not immediately think of heroin, because he viewed the addicts at the Chongqing Guest House as brainless idiots destroying their lives. I could not believe that he would imitate conduct he denounced as stupid.

"Drugs?", I finally asked.

"Commander Huang's son gave me a hit, and I became addicted." He admitted he was on drugs for about six months. I had difficulty believing this truth.

I asked him what he intended to do about it. He promised to quit, and begged me to forgive him. I told him I would give him one chance. If I saw him using again, I would disappear forever. I could not babysit him 24/7. If he wanted to play with fire, he could do it on his own time.

The next morning, when he went to the project site, I stayed behind in the hotel room. I found a pack of Kent cigarettes on the desk. I opened it and saw some white powder in it. I emptied the box in the toilet without hesitation. When Virtuous came back, he looked for the box, could not find it, and asked me whether I saw it. I told him I threw it away.

"That's a lot of money!", he whined.

"I have zero tolerance for the use of drugs, I hate drugs. If I see you touch the stuff one more time, you will never see me again."

He understood, correctly, there would be no money for drugs coming from me.

To give him spiritual support and help him quit drugs, I stayed with him - although I felt that there was a corpse sleeping in the other bed.

In the evening, I saw him painfully struggle with the effects of drug addiction. I insisted that he had to prove to me that he was still a tough man. I had no respect or sympathy for drug addicts.

A few days later, Commander Huang and a friend came to Dalian. They invited me and Susan to spend the weekend in the friend's hometown, Bin Yu Gou, a breathtakingly beautiful place. Susan encouraged me to go and leave Virtuous at the hotel.

The bucolic scenes were extremely charming, but I was worried about Virtuous. I told Susan that Virtuous was trying to shake off drug addiction. Though sympathetic, she asked me why I had not dumped him earlier for all the years of suffering he had caused. I did not know how to answer.

I knew that I no longer loved him, because I no longer respected him - though I never uttered a word of insult. I became addicted to taking care of him, a habit as dangerous as the use of narcotic. I could not imagine how he could make a living without me. How would he survive? How would he obtain the money to buy food, shelter, clothing?

When we returned to Dalian, Virtuous told me that he had broken the addiction - he did look better. I believed him. Then we went back to Shenzhen together for the 1995 Spring Festival holidays.

One night, when we were in the bedroom, Virtuous said he wanted to smoke in the living room. I sensed something was wrong, because he always smoked wherever he wanted. I surprised him in the living room - surprised and in shock, he turned off the light.

He stood up and asked, "What do you want to do?"
"Switch on the light."
He became angry and tried to prevent me from reaching the switch. We fought in the dark.

"If you do not let me switch on the light, then there must be a ghost."
"Yes, there is a ghost."
He left for the bedroom, and I turned on the light. I saw a piece of foil and a line of white powder on the glass table. I threw them in the toilet and went back into my bedroom. From the living room I heard a desperate voice, shouted:
"Where is the stuff gone?"
"I flushed it in the toilet."
"That's a lot of money!"

I did not want to talk to him anymore. I decided to leave him without bringing anything with me but a credit card. The second day, a client called and asked me to fly to Dalian right away. So I packed and left Shenzhen the same day.

After finished my work in Dalian, I told Virtuous in a phone call we were done forever and please leave me in peace. I hung up the phone before he responded.

Then I flew to Chengdu to celebrate my 28th birthday with friends and classmates. Chengdu had changed a lot since my last visit. Many high rises were under construction. I realized that it was a good time to open a branch there, so we could provide our high-quality kitchen equipment to the expanding market, not only in Chengdu, but also in its neighboring cities.

I BECOME CHAIRWOMAN OF THE BOARD

So I proposed the idea of a branch to my boss Mr. Tang. He brought his three regional managers in charge of his Singapore, Hong Kong and Shenzhen companies, respectively, to Chengdu. Upon investigating the market, they agreed that it was the right time and place to open a new branch - with a big showroom - in Chengdu.

However, Mr. Tang wanted me to be in charge of this branch. I thought I was not ready because I enjoyed traveling around and did not like to be chained to a desk. He asked me my age. I told him that I was 28. He then told me that a 28-year old woman was mature enough to run this business.

He further encouraged me by telling me that I was smarter than his three regional managers. I did not believe him, because those three people were my role models in this industry, and I respected their professionalism.

Their combined experience in this business was significant, and I was not confident without their support.

Mr. Tang reiterated he wanted me to supervise this branch, and would make the other three managers my consultants. He requested them to provide support, and based on this, I accepted the position.

So, I invested 40% of the equity needed to register this company. Mr. Tang invested the remaining 60% of the equity needed, but he asked for four board seats to which I agreed.

We rented the second floor of a two-floor building on the People's Road, one of the two major arterials in Chengdu. The location was between Chairman Mao's statue and the airport.

The first floor was a car dealership owned by Xie Xiang, the youngest son of the party secretary of Sichuan province and my neighbor.

Our showroom displayed high quality commercial and home kitchen equipment. We recruited staff and trained them during showroom construction. My eldest brother History was recruited as the vice president.

On the opening day, we had invited regulators, related government officials, presidents of hotels and friends for a cocktail party in the showroom.

Our guests brought numerous flower baskets, and the Chengdu TV station carried news of the opening. It was quite an exciting experience for me and my colleagues.

Almost at once, our business prospered and became more and more busy due to accelerated economic development. Virtuous still chased me everywhere whenever he had time. I was not happy when he disturbed my work, and told our security guards to stop him.

He then chose to sit on the staircase, waiting for me to finish work. To get rid of him, I gave him money to set up a vehicle repair business, hoping he could leave me in peace.

He took the money and found a place about three kilometers away from my office on the same road. This separated me from my 'tail'. Indeed, my old colleague, Ms. Qiu, the girl who introduced me to my boss Mr. Tang, used to call Virtuous the 'tail'.

Whenever she saw me alone, she would ask,
"What have you done with your 'tail'?"
"Why do you call him that?"
"He dragged behind you all the time - like a 'tail'."

THE ASIAN FINANCIAL CRISIS

Immediately upon the return to China of Hong Kong in 1997, Hong Kong became a victim of the Asian Financial Crisis. Contraction of monetary policy caused our headquarters in Hong Kong to downsize. It stopped delivering the goods that our Chengdu branch had ordered and paid the full amount in advance. It made me anxious, because I could not fail our clients who supported us for many years.

Our inability to finish the projects might cause our good friends to lose their jobs. So I tried hard to contact my boss Mr. Tang about this crisis, but he avoided my calls. Worries, I mentioned his unresponsiveness to my friend Nice at an occasion. Nice was sympathetic for me and asked whether Mr. Tang had children. He had four daughters.

"Kidnap one of his daughters to force him to deliver the goods. Do you need help?"

Looking at her beautiful face and classy dress, I thought - WOW! Maybe she is a tiger woman!

Inspired by her, I went back to office and faxed Mr. Tang a letter telling him that I was not willing to play hide and seek with him anymore. I gave him a deadline for delivering the equipment. If he failed me, I would cease looking for him and let a 'professional firm' in Hong Kong explain to him the necessity of coughing up the money.

However, I still made the last call and found him at home. When he answered the phone, my hot temper peppered him with questions. No matter how rude my manner, Mr. Tang, to his credit, still responded like a gentleman.

"Miss Deng, of your many correct points, only one stuck with me. That is when you said, 'how can we fail our friends who have supported us for years?' Yes, we should not do that. For this reason, I will try my best to deliver some of the goods, but I will have to leave the remainder of the problem for you to solve. That's the best I can do."

I accepted his good faith attempt to comply.

I finished the project perfectly, but with much less profit than expected, because the closure of our Shenzhen factory caused double overhead. I had to locate four new vendors in different cities to fabricate the fixtures we used to produce in one factory. This became a long and complicated commercial battle. I was relieved when the project passed the examinations in the end of 1998, and it went into operation.

1998 was stressful enough, but 1999 became a year of a real drama. I will tell the full story later in another chapter. This story alone can make a feature film.

In January 2000, a former client introduced North-Eastern Security Company as a potential client. The vice president, Ms. Jin, invited me to meet with her and her colleagues in Dalian before the Spring Festival. I agreed.

Before I flew to Dalian, Ms. Jin told my colleague that her daughter was about to have her birthday and she requested me to purchase an Omega watch for her. I bought the watch and gave it to Ms. Jin when we were having dinner at the hotel I stayed. Ms. Jin did not pay me the money for the watch, but paid for the very expensive dinner, almost the equivalent to the price of the watch. It would be reimbursed by her company anyway.

While we were eating, Ms. Jin said, "The communist party is genuinely strong, we consume it like this, it still doesn't collapse, and get stronger and stronger each year." She thought this comment hilarious, intended to demonstrate Party pride. All her colleagues joined in the laughter, proudly!

BOYFRIEND TRANSPLANT

HIT BY A ROCK

When our Chengdu Branch started in 1995, my old colleague from the cruise line recommended Charm, a beautiful 26 year-young veteran of the People's Liberation Army, to work for me. Her 'virtues' mirrored her name. I hired her as the assistant to the sales manager. She could drink men under the table, so ran interference for me when I was asked to compete in the tiresome Chinese game of who can consume the most alcohol. In China, as we have seen, this was a key indicator of potential business succes.

Charm was an active girl, and had many friends who were the sons of high officials. She told her 'friends' that her boss was a young woman. Not believing this, these 'friends' asked to meet me in person. Thus, Charm begged me many times to meet her 'friends' claiming it would be good for our business. So, on one particular day, I complied.

We first went to the office of Sunny, who was the son of the vice governor of Sichuan province. Sunny ran an import and export business, and he had friends who were the sons of the the Chinese Customs potentates.

Rock, one of them, was in town on his business trip. He worked for the company which managed all the assets of the 11th Banchan Lama. His father, who used to work in Tibet, now ran Shenzhen Custom.

Since my imported goods passed through Shenzhen Custom frequently, I asked Rock to give us a hand when we needed it. He responded, "My pleasure, anytime." So we enjoyed our meeting and expected to have more fun together.

After I met these 'friends,' I flew to Shenzhen. Rock picked me up at the airport, greeting me with a big grin. During the days following, he took me to several dinner and karaoke parties with his friends. He was apparently proud to have me as his friend, and we gradually became closer.

A few months later, it was again birthday. I invited myself to my best friend Jasmine's home. She prepared a good dinner for my birthday, but teased me I should have spent the evening with a man, instead of her. I joked she must be my temporary boyfriend since I did not have one.

She asked me, "Don't you have any suitor?"

"No", I admitted.

Just at that moment my cell phone rung and it was Rock, asking me where I was.

Jasmine began her cross examination:

"Boy or girl?"

"Married or single?"

I then remembered that Rock had told me his mother's complaint about his single, playboy status.

Jasmine, who was listening on the phone call, commanded,

"Go out with him, it's your birthday."

Rock overheard this and exclaimed,

"What? It is your birthday? Have I such good luck? Let me take you to a special place tonight."

So Rock collected both of us and took us to an exotically furnished tea house, with elegantly dressed service girls and a cricket that would sing on command. A girl performed the tea ceremony for us, and taught us how to enjoy it. The scent of the tea was pleasant, the tea sets delicate, but ridiculously overpriced.

I could not understand, but Jasmine, who had more experience from her police work, told me that the tea at her boss' office costs almost one thousand dollars per kilogram. That was more than an average Chinese person's annual income!

Jasmine and Rock discussed various topics, from tea to real estate, to the stock market. It looked to me that Jasmine, for a policewoman, had very broad knowledge. I could only listen in wonder. Then Rock took us back to Jasmine's home and left.

After Rock left, Jasmine continued her cross-examination, asking me everything about Rock's background. I told her everything I knew about him.
"Why don't you date him?"
"First, I don't really know him; second, he did not pursue me."
Then she catalogued his virtues and proclaimed that I should consider him.

I had no special feeling for Rock. I was still numb from the Virtuous debacle, testing my new wings of freedom with the old ones still clipped to the bone. I knew this Rock hung out with beautiful young girls and I did not need another playboy. However, Jasmine convinced me, though he had not expressed feelings for me, he must like me a lot because his courtship-like treatment. She encouraged me to go for this guy.

One night, Rock invited me to a ballroom dance and asked me where my boyfriend was.

"About which one are you asking?"

"How many do you have?"

"I will need some time to figure that out."

"Since you have so many boyfriends, one more would not be a burden. I am in."

Even though slow and backward in the realm of romance, it dawned on me that he was interested in me,

Eventually, I accepted Rock as my boyfriend without formally telling him so. He became my man in Shenzhen, and he tried his best to entertain and take care of me whenever I came home.

LOVE MATURED?

My busy job entailed a lot of travel, and Rock behaved supportively. Every time, I asked him to do something for me, he always did it perfectly, no matter whether it was personal or business errand.

Since my time in Shenzhen was limited, I always saw Jasmine and Rock together. Our relationship was based more on friendship rather than upon the compulsive behaviors that characterized my time with boyfriend #1. I still had bitterness about men, and no longer trust them as I did before.

About a year later, Rock came to my home and asked me to marry him. His rational was that his parents were visiting, emphasized he could not continue as a playboy, and had duty to produce grand children.

I told him that I would consider it. He then warned me not to take too long because he could not wait.

The next day, when Jasmine and I were having coffee at a Hotel, I told her about Rock's proposal. I thought I might as well marry him unless she could reveal something extremely bad about him.

She then became angry and told me,
"You can not marry him because I don't think you really love him. Every time when you came back, you spent more time with me instead of him."

Then she said, to my amazement, "Rock had expressed to me multiple times that he truly loves me, and, I found myself in love with him too. Every time, when we were together and Rock called you on phone, I became very jealous."

To prove she was not lying, Jasmine said she would call Rock and offer to have dinner with him, so we could monitor his response. I thought it was a good test, so I let her do it. She called, and Rock responded, "Good, I will pick you up after work then." So, we kept chatting until Rock called her again.

She picked it up and told him, "I am in a coffee shop with Jin Lan, would you join us?" Rock declined.

I could not enjoy this particular dinner and returned home. I called Rock and told him that I had made my decision. I said that I realized that we could only be friends, or like sister and brother, no longer lovers. He could not understand why, felt offended, but said that he respected my decision.

Rock, who claimed he could not sleep well the night before, came to my office the day after. He asked why I had come to the decision rejecting him. I told him that my decision was good for him, because after I got out of the way, he may have a true love life.

He pretended that he did not understand. I then told him that Jasmine confessed to me she was in love with him, and I thought he loved her too. He was surprised, but the gray color on his face was gone. He became a happy man and complimented me,
"You are a much more mature woman than I expected. I thought if I dumped you, you would commit suicide."

Then, Jasmine and I spent the 1997 New Year holiday traveling around Shanghai, Hangzhou and Suzhou, the three most beautiful cities in China. On the shore opposite the Bund, there was no light except the TV tower. We took a photo in front of the River and the tower. We knew our lives were growing better day by day, but we could never imagine what kind of change was coming to China.

During the trip, our discussions centered on Rock. I told her I had already broken up with Rock and would let them develop their relationship. She confessed to me that she had fallen in love with Rock at the first sight, and would be jealous if she saw me with Rock together. So I understood that she was truly in love, and promised not to go back to Rock.

Although sometimes I missed Rock, I had great sympathy for Jasmine and did not contact him. Since it is hard for anyone to find true love, if such a rare phenomenon occurred between my best friend and my then boyfriend, I should not stand in their way. I couldn't treat him like a gold claim, first-finder's keeper. I think that mutual true love is the most important criterion between two people.

She then asked me whether I thought she was selfish. I told her 'no' and I admired her honesty and courage in telling me the truth at the right time. Since then, I have not heard anything about Rock from Jasmine. I do not know what happened to them. I had never asked her, because I don't want to invade their privacy.

MY NEXT PORT OF CALL: A PIRATE SMUGGLER

A THIRD BOYFRIEND

So, in the summer of 1997, Jasmine felt sorry for me, and asked her colleagues from the police bureau to introduce some potential partners. Her chief even introduced me to a Hong Kong mafia head. I was too dumb to realize what was going on.

One day when I was in Shenzhen, Jasmine arranged a hotpot party for me. [34]

It was the usual Sichuanese hotpot joint with boiling spicy broth, crowded tables, loud chatter, a lot of cigarette smoke and beer drinking. Another character out of central castings, Commissar Liu, came along with several of his attendants. They were introduced to me as officers of the Gold Transportation Troop of the Armed Police Force.

After this party, Commissar Liu invited me to play tennis with his people. I thought I needed to build more muscle, and went. We were all novices, progressed slowly, and became closer over time.

One afternoon, Commissar Liu asked me to lend 50k yuan (worth about $6k USD then) for his temporary use, and sent his colleague Wave to my office to pick up the money.

---

[34] As the reader may have found out by now, most of the events I mentioned happen in various restaurants. Yes, restaurants are where social lives interconnect, since Chinese used to be starving and now it is a developing country with ample food.

MY NEXT PORT OF CALL: A PIRATE SMUGGLER

When my assistant asked Wave to sign a promissory note, he was so scared and refused to sign. I could not understand why, and presumed he did not want to be involved in legal paperwork.

He explained that it was not he did not want to sign; he was functionally illiterate and ashamed of it. I was surprised and asked why such an apparently smart man could not write. He then told me of the hardships he experienced during his childhood in Henan province.

Wave had never finished primary school, because his mother became mentally disordered when he was in first grade. His mother could neither take care of herself, nor recognize her own kids or husband. Wave had to care for his three younger brothers while his father was working. After doctors gave up on his mother, his family had to resort to necromancy.

They invited a witch to drive the evil spirit out of her body. Every evening, when it was dark, the witch would conduct a ritual recitation of verbal charms to produce magic effects on Wave's mother. Then the witch would burn a piece of paper and threw the ashes into a bowl of water. Thereafter, it was Wave's duty to bring this bowl of water to a remote rural area, and dump it into the realm of ghosts.

He said that though the road to this place was unlit, during one of those trips he saw his classmate's dead sister. I thought it might be the creation of a terrified mind. He performed this ritual for three plus years; his mother gradually returned to normal and loved him dearly since then. However, since he missed so many classes, he could not catch up, dropped out of school, and started working at a very young age. Wave's story was incredible to me and I was touched. I decided to tutor him. He loved this idea and said that he would come to my office to study whenever he had time. Later, the tutoring relationship became something closer when my first ex-boyfriend showed up to bother me.

DEATH OF A BLACK SWAN

By this tim, we must remember that the Asian Financial Crisis was ongoing. Besides everything becoming cheaper, I realized the depth of this crisis when I saw a beautiful young girl jump off the 24th floor of an adjoining building before my eyes. The details of this suicide never left my mind.

One weekend, when my maid Lily was cleaning the windows on the porch, she pointed to a window from our neighbor tower and exclaimed,

"Someone wants to jump off the building!"

I followed her finger and saw a young pretty girl with very white skin in a beautiful black dress. This lonely figure perched on the concrete overhang of a window at about 24th floor, and a huge crowd of people watched her from the street.

I was worried and could not understand why such a young girl had abandoned hope in this world. Lily went down to the street to find out what was happening. When she came back, she told me the girl had been on the overhang of the window since 3:00 p.m., and it was now almost 9:00 p.m. Since she had been there for six hours, she was in obvious

MY NEXT PORT OF CALL: A PIRATE SMUGGLER 133

doubt about death. Why had no one done anything constructive during those six hours?

At around 9:30 p.m., Wave came to my home. He walked to the window and cried loudly,

"She is going to jump now, come here, give me your camera, give me your camera!"

I walked to the window but refused to give him my camera. This should have warned me of a degraded spirit, but I was clueless.

I observed the girl's leap from the building, her beautiful body first arched like a ballet dancer, then spinning through the air. Her black dress billowed like the wings of a black swan. Her body hit an air bag placed on the roof of the 6th floor. It was supposed to save her. However, since it was over inflated, she catapulted off the roof of the 6th floor, and landed in the street.

So many people observed her hopeless jump, the loss of a precious, beautiful life. The show over, people vacated the street within ten minutes, leaving this girl's lonely corpse for three hours until an agarse came.

ANOTHER CHEATER

Before the Spring Festival of 1998, Wave and I started dating. Then he was sent to a business trip to Chengdu. He told me that he was going to spend the Spring Festival with me and my Mom in Shenzhen. I missed him during the long holidays, because he did not return. Spring Festival had passed by the time that he did. After that, Wave drove to Chengdu a lot, along with his colleagues. Since his troop was called Gold Transportation Troop, I never suspicted his activities.

One day, when I was working in my Chengdu office, a girl called and asked whether Wave was there, I told her he was supposed to arrive in a few minutes. The girl then asked me whether I was his girlfriend. Upon affirming this unhappy fact, she repeated the mantra that she was his girlfriend too. Shades of the non-Virtuous Virtuous.

She told me that Wave dropped her at a company that they were visiting, told her that he had to go to toilet, then disappeared. This made her angry; she believed he was coming to my office and called me. She told me that she had all my phone numbers. She must have raided his wallet while they were sleeping together. I had no reason to doubt her veracity.

While she and I were on phone, Wave walked into my office. I looked at his face and knew he had cheated on me. I was very mad at him, because, once again, I was not prepared for betrayal. I thought I treated him well, so he should behave accordingly, but he had no control over the one-eyed snake when a warm burrow beckoned.

He felt sorry and apologized to me by kowtowing on the ground like an earthworm about to be ground underfoot. He begged for another chance. I told him that I would give him only one more chance, and if he played games again, I would dump him forever. Then, we went back to Shenzhen togther.

A few weeks later, Wave said that he had to go to Chengdu for another business trip and assured me that he would never see that Chengdu girl anymore. I trusted him once again and he left. When Wave came back from the trip, he had an ashen face. Then, his Chengdu girlfriend called me on my cell phone.

The girl asked me to warn him to run as far away as fast as he could, out of the country if possible, because the cops were hunting him. If he was caught, he could be sentenced to death for defrauding the government of substantial custom taxes. I could not believe this, and asked for the full story. She told me that Wave smuggled 40 brandnew Toyota Prado jeeps to Chengdu, and was apprehended red-handed by 300 armed policemen at a small train station near that town.

However, the police could not arrest him, because he was not an ordinary citizen, but a member of the armed force. So, they invited Wave to their offices to take an affidavit. He told the police he had to go to toilet first. The police allowed him to do so because his car had been impounded, and they thought he could not escape without it. He did escape, though, in the presence of 300 policemen. The girl told me that the police was looking for me, too, and wanted to arrest me as well.

Although I hated Wave's dishonesty, stupidity and disloyalty, I did not want him to be killed. He later told me that he was commanded by Commissar Liu to do all these things. He claimed he had no other choice but to obey the order.

Smuggling was a popular crime in China for a long time; one could find smuggled cars all over the country. Some small towns, like Zhengcheng, did nothing but trade in smuggled cars. However, every so often, the government would shut down the trade and collect revenues from smuggling businesses, just like it would shut down the small, non-Mafia controlled whorehouses from time to time. The Mafia controlled ones were smart enough to have the police as partners. Wave rode the crest - so to speak - of an anti-smuggling campaign. On the run, he could not go back to his troop. I had to employ him to do my errands, since he had nowhere else to go and no income.

While hiding from the Chengdu police, Wave caused much trouble for me without cessation. So we broke up, but still kept a friendly relationship. I should have known he was poison from the day I met him.

No matter his crimes, I could never imagine that some day, I would risk my life to save him from two bullets in the back of the head, and Dance with Wolves a second time.

THE PIRATE IN CHAINS

A HOOK DINNER?

One day during June 1999, Wave was sent to Beijing by me to deal with some residual businesses for our client. He flew into Beijing and checked in the hotel that my company booked and prepaid for him. He stayed there for a week, but could not get anything done. I thought he was playing there and just making excuses. Therefore, I flew to Beijing and met with him at the hotel.

Then, his cell phone rung and it was my neighbor from Shenzhen, Sharp. Wave had told me Sharp was a former marine captain who lived in my building, where they had met. Sharp told Wave that he was in Beijing and invited us to his new house in downtown Beijing for dinner. So we attended.

Here, we were presented this big feast at Sharp's house, attended by his local friends. Someone knocked on the door. A cop came in and sat down. It was strange to me because it did not look like a friend visit. The cop did not eat. In about three minutes, he excused himself but promised to come back soon. When he returned, two other policemen accompanied him.
One of the two cops asked, "Who is Wave?"
"I am."
"Then you are the one."

The two cops were from Chengdu, showed their IDs and an arrest warrant of Wave. Everyone was shocked into silence. They arrested him and left the house. I came to life, ran to the door and stopped them. I asked them to show their IDs to me again and wrote down their names and cell phone numbers.

Of course, some of the dinner guests knew the whole story. The reason why Wave was arrested was because he asked a car dealer, who bought some smuggled cars from him, to pay money owed to him. The car dealer did not want to pay, so bribed the police to arrest him.

I was told that the owner of the car dealer was a middle-aged woman and the classmate of the police chief of Chengdu. That was why she had the guts to make money by buying so many smuggled cars. Her cover was she pretended to import parts and use them to assemble autos at her plant. In fact, she and her son Beyond, purchased smuggled cars from Sharp and Wave, instead.

Sharp bragged that he had a contract to sell 400 smuggled cars with Beyond, that they used to be like brothers. Sharp was about 28 years old, a government official's son. He actually owned a luxury house at a rich neighborhood of Shenzhen, in addition to his new house in Beijing, and the Shenzhen condo in the same building with mine.

I do not know whether he exaggerated the number of cars, but I believe he made big money from smuggling them into China[35]. Otherwise, there could be no other reason he

---

[35] Custom tax rate for imported cars was 220% in 1992. With continuing deregulation, it reduced to 80-100% by 2000, but left enough profit space to incentivize a lot of people to break the law, although it did protect the development of automobile industry. According to Wu Song Quan:
http://www.catarc.ac.cn/upload/www/201901/171600577xim.pdf

could accumulate so much money at his age since he was not otherwise talented.

The 40 Toyota jeeps shipped by Wave and intercepted by the Chengdu Police were supposed to be sent to Beyond. When the police were rounding up the related parties in the smuggle case, Beyond, terrified, ran to Shenzhen where he had a house. However, due to his terror and stress, he crashed into a tree in the center of the town and died.

He was only 25 and his mother's only son. When Wave tried to collect the payment from Beyond's mother, she was angry and would not pay. So, she called the police chief to arrest Wave. In fact, later, the cops who arrested Wave, told my lawyer that Beyond's mother paid them the travel expenses to arrest Wave in Beijing. She told them that Wave had to die to accompany her son in the ground.

I totally understood both her grief for her son and her hatred of Wave. However, Beyond's mother knew that her company had not assembled those cars. She was the only one with the political connections to give those smuggled cars legalized identities.

HELP

Wave and the two cops were on the airplane to Chengdu in the same evening. I went back to my hotel and called a powerful friend to help. I asked him to tell the cops in Chengdu not to beat Wave, because I saw how Virtuous was beaten by the police in Chongqing.

The second day, I called several friends to brainstorm solutions to save Wave. They told me that I'd better talk with them in person. So, I withdrew all the cash I had in a bank in Beijing and flew back to Shenzhen. Banks then were not connected nationally.

At my Shenzhen home, I dug into Wave's suitcase, found a contract between Wave's troop and the Chengdu company owned by Beyond's mother. It was signed by Beyond and had an official military stamp of Wave's troop. I then called my high school dormmate Red Guard, a lawyer who worked for the Shenzhen Court as a judge and asked her to help.

After I told her about Wave's case, she said that the amount of unpaid custom taxes was enough to justify a death sentence eight times over. Thus, a trial would guarantee two bullets in the back of the head. She suggested I should obtain Wave's release on bail before trail and help him escape abroad. I asked her to recommend a good lawyer in Chengdu. She referred Quiet, who was the law school classmate of the attorney general in Chengdu.

Then, I met with my best friend Jasmine and discussed how to save Wave.
"I know you, if you don't save Wave, you won't sleep well, even though he betrayed you, and you have already broken up."
"If I don't try to save his life, no one else will."

She understood that I just had sympathy for Wave as a human being, and nothing more. So, she suggested that commissar Liu should be held responsible for the smuggling, because it was he who sent Wave to Chengdu. We both believed that if Wave was taking the orders from commissar Liu, then it was a conspiracy for which Wave should not take sole responsibility.

Yet, we did not have any evidence to prove commissar Liu was the real brains and power behind the crime. Jasmine suggested I call commissar Liu, invite him for breakfast, and secretly record our discussion. So, I could use this evidence to prove a conspiracy.

The next morning, I invited commissar Liu for breakfast. I did not record him, but I blamed him for commanding Wave to engage in smuggling, a charge which he denied. He told me that Wave betrayed him by doing all these behind his back. I did not know who was lying; perhaps both of them.

Though I hated Wave, I did not believe that he deserved to die. I could not think of a reason commissar Liu let Wave leave Shenzhen for so long, unless he had his consent. So, I told commissar Liu, "I saw a contract about the cars between your troop and the Chengdu car dealer."

"I don't believe it."

"The contract has the stamp of your troop on it."

"I would like to help Wave, but I really can't do anything, it was all Wave's fault."

"If so, I will provide the police the contract in order to save Wave's life, if you don't do anything to help."

"I did not do anything wrong. I have no fear."

"The contract I saw clearly stated that your troop is responsible for the transportation of a number of cars for a Chengdu car dealer, from Zhengcheng to Chengdu. It provided that it was the car dealer's duty to present the legal documents. Although it doesn't have your signature, it has your troop's stamp on it." To this point, he did not reply.

When I returned home, I thought about Wave in jail and his approaching death. I could not sit and do nothing.

Sleepless, watching the roof at night, time was bleeding, I could hear his life ticking away. I decided to fly to Chengdu right away.

TWO BULLETS FLY BY

A MAGICIAN WITH A BAG OF CASH

When I landed in Chengdu with a bag of cash, my friend Vanilo picked me up at the airport. I told him all I knew about Wave's case. He said he would ask his sister's fiancé, the No. 2 leader in the Sichuan Province Police Force, to look into the situation. He wanted to discover whether Wave could be bailed out, so he could escape. He suggested that we organize a dinner together the next day to hear this gentleman's feedback.

I checked into a hotel and called jail cop Fly who I befriended while my first boyfriend, Virtuous, was in jail. When I asked his help, he offered his support. I asked him to find jail cops to arrange communication with Wave, and he brought two of them to have dinner with me.

At the dinner, they told me that there were Jails #1 and #2 in this system. Once transferred to Jail #1, Wave would have to go to trial. Wave was still in Jail #2, this means he was still in the process of investigation.

One of the two jail cops was a young leader in charge of Jail #2. He told me that he would protect Wave so that no one would dare beat him. I gave him an envelop of cash and said that was for Wave if he needed to buy anything in the jail. He said to me, "Whatever Wave needs, I will bring to him. You will need to spend a lot of money on other occasions. So, please conserve your money now." I appreciated his generousity and kind heart.

The other young cop from Jail #1 also offered to help when needed.

I asked Fly whether he believed that there was a way to get help from the police who were working on Wave's case. He said that it was possible, since the cops who were working on this case were young, although he did not know them. I felt hopeful when I heard this, but still did not know what to do.

I had to study the case, find the key evidence proving Wave was not the instigator of the crime. Until then, I only heard the story from Wave's friend Sharp and his Chengdu girlfriend. How much truth was in their statements? I did not know yet. Fly suggested that we should visit the police office the second day.

The second morning, I went to the police office with Fly. We interviewed one of the young cops who arrested Wave in Beijing. I asked the reason for the arrested. He told me that Wave used 150 sodiers from the Armed Forces to smuggle into Chengdu 40 Toyota jeeps. The size of Wave's gang of smugglers inspired the Chengdu police to enlist 300 special policemen to catch them.

I told him that an illiterate young man was not capable of designing and executing such a scheme.
"Well, it was unlucky for him that he was captured, but had he succeeded, he would be a big man, now!" That was all he would tell me.

In the afternoon, I met with a lawyer recommended by Sharp. After my summary of the case, he told me straight that this case had no hope.
"Wave has to die, because so many people want him to die and they are all powerful. Wave is a nobody, no one will

stand out for him except you. You must give up; no matter how much money you spend, he will be killed anyway".

"Wave deserves to have a fair trial," I insisted.

"Usually, the police will not risk questioning higher-ups. As long as Wave admitted his crime, the police will close the case immediately. I know them too well."

I still could not believe that a vital young man will soon be ashes.

In the evening, Vanilo revealed he had spoken with the No. 2 police chief who knew the case. This was the largest smuggling case of Sichuan province in 1998, covered by newspapers and TV everywhere; even the central the government had been notified.

In view of this vast publicity, the case would be expedited and bail would be impossible. Wave had been caught red-handed.

I was disappointed. However, I still determined to find the best lawyer to save Wave's life. I recalled that my high school classmate, Red Guard, had given me another source, a lady attorney named Quiet.

I HAVE A STROKE OF LUCK

I visited Quiet's office located in the attorney general's building. She was in her 50's and kind to me. After describing Wave's case, I asked her what I should do to save him. She comforted me.

During this recitation, I broke into tears, and Quiet told me that she admired my support for Wave. She was amazed that an ex-girlfriend would provide such support. She stated even married couples would not be so loyal. I simply replied there was no one else on the planet would/could save his life.

Attorney Quiet said she would visit Wave in jail as soon as possible and asked whether I would visit him with her. I had no desire to see him. Though all the romantic feelings had vanished, the fate had put me between him and death.

At about this time, one of her associates, a male lawyer named Brilliance came into the room and asked who was in charge of the case.
"Someone named Peak," I replied.
A big smile came over his face.

He told Quiet there might be something that could be done. Then he asked me to return the next day for further discussions. Before leaving, I paid them a big retainer for legal consultancy. Two large smiles appeared on their faces. It was big money in 1999's China, but I would have spent my last dime to achieve a just result. They both comforted me,
"Don't worry, we will find a way to save his life."

PULLING THE TIGER'S SKIN[36], CASE I

The next day, Wave's boss, commissar Liu called me on phone.
"How is the situation in Chengdu?"

---

[36] This is a stragem to use a powerful individual's name to imply you are a part of the power, so it may help obtain favors and deter predators. This strategy is commonly practiced in Chinese businesses.

"Everyone here told me that Wave must die if there is no other evidence prove he is not the principle criminal."

To save Wave's life, I threatened to go to the police with their contract, " I am on my way to deliver the contract between your troop and the Chengdu car dealer, because it may prove that Wave was not the only smuggler in this case - but just doing his duty assigned by you."

"No, please don't do this. I will find a way to help."

I told him he could help by affixing his signature to the contract. This was a bold suggestion, but he agreed to do so.

He went to my office in Shenzhen and signed the original copy of the contract and faxed a copy to my hotel in Chengdu. To my amazement, Commissar Liu had signed not his, but his commander's name. I was upset and called him on phone.

"Why did you change your mind again? It's not your name."

"The commander agreed to help Wave, and authorized me to affix his name. If the police want to investigate, they may reach him."

Ordinary cops couldnot reach the commander since he was always guarded by soldiers; people knew his father was one of the generals in the PRC. With his support, I felt confident that I might be able to save Wave's life.

Later that day, commissar Liu asked for my bank account number and deposited about $5,000 dollars worth of RMB into my bank account to assist Wave. I accepted this, because I believed that he should be responsible for Wave's defense. If he and his commander were not guilty as well, they would not have sent a dime. Their PRC salaries were minimal.

LIGHT AT THE END OF THE TUNNEL

I brought the faxed contract to attorney Quiet's office. She and Brilliance were both waiting for me. Brilliance revealed that Peak had been his law school classmate.

Peak told him that Wave admitted everything, and they were about to close this case. Wave's destiny was a death sentence had we not reached Peak, because Wave's death would ensure the promotion of Peak's boss, Beyond's mother wanted Wave in a grave next to her son. Moreover, the police had a slam dunk case because they had 40 jeeps and Wave's confession.

Here in Chengdu, except myself, no one else would be eager to see Wave stay alive. Brilliance told Peak that I would do anything I could to save Wave. Peak was amazed and said that he really admired my courage, loyalty and generosity.

Brilliance, "Peak could not believe that you two are not married. He knew that Wave had betrayed you for another girl. He spied on her for a long time to catch Wave."

Brilliance: "He also understood that smuggling is the norm of this society. He was paid by Beyond's mother to arrest Wave in Beijing. At the same time, he totally knew that the buyer of the 40 jeeps was the company owned by Beyond's mother."

After Brilliance provided this intelligence, I showed him the fax which proved Wave was not the principle of the crime. He made a copy of this and said he would bring it to Peak.

In further analyzing the case, we realized there must be evidence of substantial financial transactions between the buyer and the seller of the smuggled cars. We decided to get the evidence to support our assumption. So we went to the car dealer's place to check their formal company names. This car dealer had several business licenses and we wrote down all of its company names.

The day after, with the contract in hand, Brilliance asked his brother in law, who was a captain of an anticrime branch of the police, to obtain the car dealer's bank records from the central bank of China. His brother in law had the authority to obtain these records, and securied copies of suspected wire transactions in two days.

The contract and the wire transfer records supported our assumption that the real seller of the smuggled cars was someone else. Wave's troop only made income from transporting goods from city A to city B. If the troop's transportation of these cars represented an illegal act, then the railway company, which transported those 40 jeeps from Guangdong to Sichuan, must be culpable too.

Brilliance and I became excited about these findings; he believed that by showing our evidence we could not only save Wave's life, but also obtain his release in one month.

Suddenly, Brilliance said to me, "You have to move to another hotel right now, because Beyond's mother might hire killers to murder you, once she finds out you have evidence of her crimes and are determined to save Wave at the potential cost of her freedom."

He then said, "This evidence can put her in jail forever, if not guarantee a death sentence, unless she can bribe someone on high to save her."

I switched hotels every day since that day. I did not even tell Brilliance where I was staying, in case he leaked the information unintentionally. Everytime, I met with him in different place to throw off potential spies.

Brilliance brought the copies of our findings to Peak. They eliminated the pressure from his boss and Beyond's mother to close the case and execute Wave. The evidence we presented to Peak suggested that the real story was different than what they surmised.

Brilliance told me that acording to Chinese law, after seven days of detention, if the police still do not have enough evidence of probable cause to support their charges, they may apply to the attorney general for another 30 days' extension of detention. After 37 days, if the police still had insufficient evidence to prosecute, they had to release Wave.

Then I learned from Brilliance that Wave was not arrested, but under custody. In fact, Wave had been illegally detained. The notice of detention authorized in the summer of 1998, had expired, but no one had extended the date. I began to be over optimistic and expected that Wave could leave the jail soon. So, I gave Brilliance a big amount of money to bail Wave out, and told him that once the charges were dismissed, the money will become his bonus. He thanked me and left with the cash.

In the following weeks, I thought that Wave would be released, but it did not occur. Beyond's mother and Peak's boss would not let it happen. With the evidence from the bank, the police could have arrested Beyond's mother, because title to the 40 jeeps was in her company name, and on the railway lading bill. Also, its wire transfer to the uperstream seller proved its relationship with her.

However, Peak's boss determined to send Peak to Shenzhen to arrest the seller, instead of arresting the buyer in Chengdu. Brilliance told me to call commissar Liu to direct the seller, who had a foreign identity, never come to China. I called commissar Liu, and he said that the seller disappeared long before and could not be found.

Peak and his colleague spent a week in Shenzhen, enjoyed their trip, but came back empty handed. Now I demanded Wave be released, because the 37-day legal detention cap had run.

A PREMATURE CELEBRATION

The result surprised all of us. The Chengdu People's Procuratorate illegally arrested Wave, and he was transferred to Jail # 1 because Beyond's mother bribed the attorney general. She was worried that once Wave got out of jail, he might hurt her. At least, this was what I heard from Brilliance. He was confident that the attorney general would never gather enough evidence to put Wave on trial and could not afford to expose Beyond's mother's crime. If the attorney general insisted, we would present our evidence to his political rival and put him in trouble.

All of us were upset about Wave's arrest, and I began to doubt Peak's effort on helping me. Then Brilliance brought Peak to meet with me, assuring, they would eventually obtain Wave's release. They asked me to be patient, because we had powerful enemies.

Peak asked me to write Wave a note assuring him he would be free. He said that Wave was extremely upset when he went to take his deposition, because his transfer to Jail #1 meant to him a death sentence.

After Wave was transferred to Jail #1, I was not in the mood for business and stopped working. I focused on getting him out of jail. His continued incarceration meant I had to get help from the people working on his case in Chengdu People's Procuratorate. Now, the attorney general's people were working up the prosecution's case. Their purpose was to put Wave on trial and ensure his execution; Beyond's mother was unrelenting.

I determined to fight her until I obtained Wave's safety. This was a long fight, and I could not stay in expensive hotels consuming money that we may need for the fight. Thus, I downgraded to cheaper hotels.

I visited the outside of Jail #1 and saw the high walls. The atmosphere was beyond depressing. I decided not to see Wave, but spoke to the young jail cop who was introduced to me by my old friend Fly. The young jail cop and his boss came out to meet me at a restaurant. I told them Wave was now in their care and needed help. They told me that it was more likely that Wave would be tried or remain there forever rather than obtaining freedom.

I did not want to believe them. So they told me that there were people in their jail for over ten years without trial. I told them that I would win my battle to release him and, until my success, please take good care of him. I gave them a stack of cash which I told them was for Wave. They said that they would make sure that Wave received the money for whatever expenses he had in prison.

I met one of the jail cops again the next weekend. He brought me a letter from Wave saying that he received the money. I doubted its authenticity because the letter made it sound as though we were still lovers, which was not true. I kept that suspicion to myself and did not comment.

Peak introduced Brilliance to the two young cops who were working for the attorney general on Wave's case. Brilliance told them our side of story, and my sincere support for Wave. The two young cops were touched and agreed to help. However, they could only passively confront their boss, since he controlled their future. They were yet another source informing me I should be careful of Beyond's mother, a crazed lioness who wanted to eat me.

Then one night, the cop in Jail #1 called me to have tea; he said he had something important to tell me. I did not know what that could be, but I knew I needed to deposit more money for Wave. However, I suspected that anyone connected with this enterprise, could be bought by Beyond's mother, and enlisted to kidnap me.

I experienced numerous cops conspiring with criminals to make money in the past. Depressing Jail #1 was a place of pure evil.

I could no longer feel safe in that city and wanted to ask a friend to accompany me to tea, but no one was in town that night. So, I called my brother Banyan who was in Chongqing, and told him to call my cell phone every five minutes pretending he was joining us for tea.

I met the Jail #1 cop at a tea house in a gloomy street. He gave me a letter allegedly written by Wave. In the letter, he thanked me for helping him and apologized for his past wrong deeds. I wrote him back at the tea house telling him to hang in there, and that I would fight for his freedom.

While I was sitting there with the Jail #1 cop, my brother Banyan kept calling me on phone and pretending to have lost directions to the tea house. I repeatedly told him the tea house address, and my location therein. When I finished writing the letter to Wave, I gave the Jail #1 cop an envelop of cash for Wave and thanked him for his assistance. I left there in darkness but safely reached my hotel.

The attorney general's cops spent another month pretending to collect more evidence. They went to Shenzhen to catch the seller, and came back, once again, empty handed. However, the attorney general refused to release Wave.

I then realized that the fight would take more time than I anticipated. Also, Beyond's mother might send someone to find me and kill me if I stayed in Chengdu long enough. So I decided to return to Shenzhen and let the lawyers work on the case. I gave my all cash to Brilliance before I left.

When I got back home, I kept searching for help to save Wave. My friends dissuaded me from this, reminding me of my futile help given the degraded Virtuous. I told them I would attempt to save the life of any human being who came into my power, but that I would stay away from jailbirds and not repeat the mistake.

While waiting for the news about Wave, I revised my life path and believed that I should make a change. However, I had no idea which direction I should go. My business partner introduced an English man, Tim Jones, to me. Tim wrote me the first love letter that listed numerous reasons why he fell in love with me, and sponsored me to visit him in London.

While waiting for my UK visa interview in Beijing, I was invited to stay at my high school classmate Happy's home. From researching on the internet to help her husband's business, she discovered a Fortune 500 paint company, Valspar. She suggested that we set up a joint venture to import their paint.

MY GODOT APPEARS

Vladimir and Estragon's Godot never appeared in the play, *Waiting for Godot*, written by Samuel Beckett in 1953. *My* Godot appeared and solved some of the problems and puzzles of my past, by opening my mind and reinterpret the meaning of love and life. He is not a fantasy, but a flesh and blood human being, a true gentleman who entered my world apparently for the purpose of rescuing my soul and enlightening me. This man enriched me with true love and liberated me in order to search for and embrace true love and life. He inspired me to see hope in every direction, and through new dimensions. Once I met him, I no longer felt insecure. I did not invent the name Godot for him, it is the birth name given him by his father, who knew and loved Western literature.

In Mandarin his name, 'Godot' means "More Songs". His father hoped China could sing more songs than the wornout melody of class struggle. So, while most 60's and 70's newborns had been given names related to the Cultural Revolution, Godot's name reminded people that art and literature could triumph over turmoil. His father was wise.

In November 1999, this adorable Shanghainese gentleman Godot was introduced to me by a girlfriend. Godot was a banker and three years younger than I was. He looked like Elvis Presley when he sang. He had a metallic voice, a pair of big round smiling eyes, long eyelashes, tall and fit, with thick sexy lips. He was a former professional basketball player from the same team that Yao Ming once belonged to.

MY GODOT APPEARS

We got to know each other by playing a card game called "tractor," with other friends.

With time, Godot and I developed mutual feelings. I realized that communication was more important for a relationship than I thought. I had a four months' communication with Tim Jones in English through internet, but it was overwhelmed by one month's communication with Godot in Chinese. Physically, they both were perfect men and I could not tell who was better. I felt sorry for Tim, because I gave up on him so quickly.

Godot had merits that a woman would dream of. He was especially sensitive about my feelings and very caring for family members. One time, I was away for a business trip in Shanghai and left my father at my Shenzhen home. When my Father had an acute back pain and called me for help, I called Godot. He went to my home and carried my Father to the hospital. Not only that, my Father told me that Godot applied the Chinese medicine for his back and massaged it until he felt much better. Who could not be touched by such a beautiful soul?

Godot and I decided to welcome the new millennium eve and watch the sunrise together. I realized that I was attached to Godot and asked his opinion about me going into the paint business. He loved this idea and supported me to go for it.

So I started the paint business with my highschool classmate Happy's husband Great China. Then the British Embassy called and indicated my UK visa was ready. I tried so hard and paid so much to get it. Now I didn't need it anymore. I was in love with Godot.

The next month, Ms. Mary Devon, the manager of the international sales department of Valspar Corporation and one director of the board, Dr. Wolf, came to Beijing. They wanted us as an agent but refused to give us the exclusive rights. This made us question about how much we should invest in the advertisement, since other distributors could take a free ride on our ads. However, we had already started the business, we could only accept what Valspar offered.

PULLING THE TIGER'S SKIN[37], CASE II

Great China encouraged me to expand our business network, so I actively participated in numerous social events. Once upon a time, Chief Li, who worked for the Third Construction Engineering Bureau of Beijing, organized a large event in Zhan Jiang, Guangdong province. He stated if I was interested in meeting with Chairman Mao's secretary Madam Zhang Yu Feng, I should join them.

I was interested in meeting Madam Zhang Yu Feng, because there were conflicting rumors about her and I was curious about what kind of woman she was. There was a rumor that she met Chairman Mao on his train and became his mistress. Yet another rumor said that she had two daughters with Chairman Mao. Others said that even Chairman Mao's wife Jiang Qing had to get her permission to visit with Mao.

---

[37] Pulling a tiger's skin is a stragem to use a powerful individual's name to imply you are a part of the power, so it may help obtain favors and deter predators. This strategy is commonly practiced in Chinese businesses.

This event was hosted by a real estate developer Mr. Lin from Shenzhen, but his project site was in Zhan Jiang. I met Mr. Lin and his beautiful young mistress in Beijing at a restaurant when Chief Li called me to join them. Mr. Lin wanted to attract public attention to his project, so his public

Madam Zhang Yu Feng in Between When Mao Meeting Nixon

relation firm designed a "Achieving Prosperity Tree Planting Event", derived from a Tang Dynasty myth about that era's Dowager Concubine Yang.

To cheer up his favorite concubine Yang, Emperor Xuan Zong sent people transporting lychee from the South to the North of China, with the fastest horses to make sure the lychee were fresh when delivered, because lychee was concubine Yang's favorite fruit.

So, to attract the public to this event, the rumor was spread that the former concubine of Chairman Mao would be planting a lychee tree to celebrate the opening. Another purpose of this strategy was to inform the local government know that the developer had a strong connection with the higher ups, so the local officials would help the project along without constantly demanding bribes.

As we know, real estate projects usually need numerous approvals and official stamps, and each approval and stamp is an avenue for corruption.

This is probably true everywhere.

When I arrived at the Beijing airport, the attendees of the Tree Planting Event were already there waiting for me. Chief Li introduced me to Madam Zhang Yu Feng and told her that I was an agent of an American paint company. Chief Li let me call her Aunt Zhang, so I did.

Aunt Zhang was such an elegant old lady that very few women of that age could match her charm. Although she had white hair, her skin looked so healthy and young. Her husband was also there, and she let me call him Uncle Liu. He looked like a movie star from Chinese films. He was tall and had a perfect, handsome, sun tanned square face, a straight back, and was always smiling when talking to people.

Our group was huge and occupied almost half of the seats on the airplane. I sat with a semi-retired government official. I knew this was intentionally arranged because chief Li wanted me to dump Godot and marry a high official.

I don't remember his name now, just remember that he once held an important office. This guy told me that his son's company owned gold mines in Northern China and was making big money.

"Where is your hometown?"

"Chongqing."

MY GODOT APPEARS

"The former party secretary Zhang De Lin of Chongqing is my close friend. I used to write him notes to get help for my friends. He could not get along with his team, so he was moved to a position in the central government, but not as practically powerful as before.

"I can still write notes to the new leaders in Chongqing if needed."

I guess he might be reminding me that he was powerful and useful. He gave me his business card. It characterized him as vice minister in rank.

When the airplane landed Shenzhen, the local government arranged limos to pick up Aunt Zhang and the other attendees. She refused to get in the Mercedes limo that was arranged for her and her husband. I didn't know whether she wanted to avoid a corruption allegation from the media. She insisted that she and her husband would go with me.

This disappointed the host Mr. Lin who felt lost face because he told the local government that Aunt Zhang was his friend, and he invited her to plant the tree.

However, Aunt Zhang asked me, "Anyone picking you up?"

"My boyfriend is right there."

"Great! Then we would love to go with you."

When we walked to the car, there was a huge bouquet of white lily flowers in the front seat.

Aunt Zhang looked at it and said, "Wow! I had never received such a big bouquet of flowers!"

Godot smiled and said, "Ha, comrade Someone is criticized."

Uncle Liu smiled and said, "Got it. My work needs to be improved."

Godot drove us to the hotel where all the guests were arranged to stay. I told him I could not have dinner with him but would see him again after dinner. He said he was at my disposal, would be around, and left.

The dinner was set at the largest VIP room of one of Shenzhen's newest and best seafood restuarants. There were so many guests we had to have several large tables. I thought I should sit with the wives of the government officials and picked a chair to sit down. However, Aunt Zhang insisted that I sit with her. So, the beautiful young mistress of the host, Mr. Lin, had to move to the other table. I sensed that Mr. Lin was quite unhappy with me, although he kept his smile.

I ignored his unhappiness that Aunt Zhang might be too interested in me, and just enjoyed my time there. When the manager of the restaurant invited us to pick the seafood for the dinner, Aunt Zhang asked me to accompany her. I did not know how she became so attached to me in so short time. I wish my readers could see the inhabitants of the fish tanks, many beautifully colored, some drab, that would soon find their way into our stomachs. We ordered almost every nice dish that the restaurant had on offer. The bill would be large, that we knew.

Sitting at the dinner, Aunt Zhang toasted us, "At such a great feast we have gathered together so many friends who are successful government officials and entrepreneurs. We entered a great era of development, and prosperity is ahead. May all your businesses thrive! Cheers!"

Then the chat became boring and corrupted. Chief Li told us that people at his unit loved gamble so much, they bet on everything including vehicle numbers and numbers on currency. He mentioned that, once, on one of his construction cites, his employees bet on bricks. They bet on whether bricks would be standing or lying down once thrown to the other side of a wall. One bet, 10,000 yuan (about $1200 USD worth in 1999).

Aunt Zhang overheard and got angry, "Where did you guys get the money for such big bet? All these guys should be arrested." Then the chatter about gambling suddenly stopped. Aunt Zhang got bored and asked, "Where is Godot?"

"He is nearby having dinner with his client for Mid Autumn Festival."

"Right, today is Mid Autumn Festival, it is a festival when all family members and lovers should be together. We should not separate you two. Call him, let him join us!"

I was surprised and looked at chief Li, the organizer. I knew he did not want to see Godot, because chief Li was trying to match me with the guy who sat by me on the airplane. He revealed this idea before, said I was a businesswoman, and if I had a powerful man to be my backbone, my business would thrive. I told him about Godot, he said, "forget about him."

Chief Li's face looked pained, but I still called Godot and he joined us in 10 minutes. Right after Godot joined us, the singers, who usually only perform in the lobby, now came into our VIP room. They sang the song, *On the Golden Mountain of Beijing*. Every Chinese knew it. It sang the praise of Chairman Mao. The song made us recall our memories of Chairman Mao's time[38].

Listening to the song, and thinking about how the people talked about Aunt Zhang behind her back, I was wondering whether she was aware of the rumors about her and Chairman Mao. When the song ended, all people in the room affectionately clapped, including Uncle Liu. He was so sincerely proud of his wife. I began to discredit the rumors about her being Chairman Mao's secret concubine.

The second day, all people flew to Zhan Jiang to watch Aunt Zhang plant the lychee tree. The media from all venues were invited to the event. The host bragged he spent several million yuan to plant this tree. Aunt Zhang pleasantly planted it capably, but she had no idea what it inferred to the public. I didn't know whether I should inform her, someday, or just let it go.

I LOSE PATIENCE

Upon my return to Beijng from the Tree Event, I kept networking for business and the thought of ways to help Wave. Attorney Brilliance kept telling me that Wave could be out in one week. Another week passed. Then another. And I learned the money I gave him before was squandered on the Majiang table by the people who controlled Wave's life. Brilliance kept asking me for more money every so often. Eventually, I lost patience and trust on him. Wave had

---

[38] Strangely, no matter how dramatic the contrast of our lives under Mao and under Deng, we didn't blame our impoverished lives on Mao, and believed that our improved lives was built on the foundation Mao laid.

spent almost two years in custody, and, though still alive, there was no resolution of his case.

So, I called Brilliance's partner attorney Quiet and told her that I would no longer send any more money. I told her to inform Brilliance, "If they want to keep Wave in jail forever, let them. I am getting married to a very good man. Please refund my money."

Quiet was surprised, "I am so sorry, I really don't know that you gave Brilliance so much money. I promise I will make sure Wave will be released soon."

I told her not to blame Brilliance, "It was my own decision, but based on the premise that Wave could be out in one week, then another week, another more week... Now, it's been almost two years, he is still in jail."

When I put down the phone, I thought, I could no longer just sit and wait. I had to go to Chengdu and check out what was happening. So, I invited a male friend from the central government to go to Chengdu with me. We flew into Chengdu and attorney Brilliance picked us up at the airport. He took us for dinner and then karaoke.

In the karaoke VIP room, two young cops from the attorney general's office were introduced to us. I introduced my friend from Beijing to them. They looked at my friend, who was wearing a belt with a national emblem, and began to worry who he might be. I told them that if they could not get Wave out of jail soon, I would like initiate formal procedures to get him out.

The two young cops said that they heard about me and revered my courage and generosity. They explained the complicated legal process and the difficulties getting around higher power intervention. Their strategy was to let the public forget about this case first, and then dismiss it. They did not want anyone to be killed now.

Beyond's mother expected Wave to be put on trial and executed. However, now she knew that if she pushed the case further, she would get herself in serious trouble. These two young cops promised me that they would get Wave out in two months, so I gave them two more months and flew back to Beijing.

DESTINED TO AMERICA?

The paint business developed slow. Until then, companies in China still had to import goods through import and export companies that had government permissions. Our company did not have the permission to import goods, so we had to import through someone who had the permission. This means that we did not have a direct contract with Valspar, and thus was buried a seed that prevented my later law suit against Valspar, when it breached the contract.

Before my first container arriving Shenzhen, a friend introduced me to Mr. Song, who was the president of another Valspar agent in China. He told me that his boss was not doing well, and the main reasons were to blame the fault of Valspar. For example, their containers were poor quality, and of plastic. He warned me that I should ask Valspar for metal containers, because they had experienced ruptured containers and paint poured on the ground of their warehouse. This product loss cost his boss a lot of money. I followed his advice and asked Ms. Mary Devon for metal cans, or better quality of plastic cans.

Mary ignored my request and insisted sending me the same containers with which other agents had issues. When my goods arrived in Shenzhen, about one hundred cans of expensive paint were ruptured. Mary Devon refused to help us to receive insurance compensation, because we did not have a direct contract with Valspar that would protect us.

Then one day during the summer of 2001, Mr. Song asked me to do him a favor. His nephew, who was living in the United States, had leukaemia. All his family members in the United States could not match the patient's bone marrow needs. Mr. Song tried to determine whether his spinal marrow was amatch for his nephew.

There was a very high American Visa rejection rate, and Mr. Song had never left the country. He decided to apply for a business visa, instead a visitor's visa. Thus, he asked me to have Mary Devon to send an invitation letter characterizing him as my vice president.

I wanted very much to help Mr. Song save his nephew's life. So, I wrote Mary Devan an email expressing our intention to visit Valspar, and told her the truth that Mr. Song needed help. She sent me the invitation, and we got our visas without any trouble.

THE PIRATE IS SAVED

Later that summer, attorney Brilliance called and told me that he could take Wave out in two days if I gave him more money for bailout.

I told Brilliance, "If you can do this, you will get all the bail money when the time is due, but I want you to tell Wave that

I am already married to someone else, and he should not make further trouble for me."

"Thank you very much for your generousity! I promise I will convince Wave not to interfere your life."

After putting down the phone, I felt relieved that Wave's life was saved, but still worried about his jealous tempermant. I called his mom and told her that her son could be home soon.

"I had tried my best to save his life, but I am married. Please tell him not to bother me anymore," I told her.

She was very happy and excited about her son's good news, "Thank you so so much! I will make sure he won't interfere your life."

Two days later, Wave knocked at my door and thanked me for saving his life. He knelt down and kowtou to me. He said his mother told him, "Your life before 37 was given by me, after today, your life has been given by Jin Lan. You should only do good things to repay her, and not to cause her more trouble."

Wave, "What can I do for you?"

Me, "I am fine and need no help."

After that day, I only saw him once, with Godot. Then I no longer kept contact with him, although he called several times and offered to bring me some gifts. I could not afford any further complication. I wanted a simple life.

A SLEEPWALKER IN AMERICA

Two months after September 11th, 2001, I visited the Eastcoast of the United States. When I walked close by Ground Zero, my heart pounded in my chest and I had feelings of sadness overlaid with horror and anger. I could think of only one word, "crazy!" After I took a boat to see the Statue of Liberty, my emotions calmed down, and the view reminded me why people love America. Yes, only if we let our anger and biases go, can we then be free.

During the visit, an American friend asked what impressed me the most about America. I considered a lot of things, then I thought the topic too serious. I didn't want to go there. So, I told him that I saw a huge billboard with two lines on it:

God Bless America
Every Box Is On Sale

As an atheist and communist, I thought that was funny. "Boxes must be expensive without God's blessing."
However, years later, I realized the truth that everything could be expensive without God's blessing, because God/the Universe/Mother Nature has set us free to create abundance and preserve justice by a set of immutable rules. Violations of these rules would be revenged by poverty, slavery, disease, wars and bad weather.

During my trip on behalf of my Mom, I visited my cousin's family in Los Altos, California. They fled mainland China for Taiwan in 1948, and lost contact for over 50 years. My cousin Success and his wife Olivia answered the door. They were happily surprised and invited me in. Olivia was a dedicated Christian, she instantly led me to the topic of God. In 15 minutes, she sensed my suspicion of biblical creation, and told me that I was brainwashed by the communisty party.

I felt insulted. How could that be? I was such a modern and worldly woman!

Only after another 15 years, did I realize how close minded I had been. No matter how truth was presented, I could not see it. In fact, this blindness is not unique to China, it afflicts all human societies. America is no exception!

Due to inefficient communication, our business with Valspar could not flourish, not did their other Chinese agents experience success. It was a completely different business culture than my experience in the commercial kitchen business, and the distance between paint manufacturer and agent was unbridgeable. So, I decided to sell my stock of paint and move on.

MY LOVER BECOMES MY BROTHER

The romantic relationship with Godot gradually evolved into a sister-brotherhood relationship, due to personal reasons. We still cared for each other as before, because the trust between us was built on a solid foundation. We did not tell his parents after we made this decision and socialized with each other without intimacy.

I started to meet some men from match.com and a Chinese matchmaker. Godot behaved as a good brother helping me to identify a potential life partner. His parents still treated me like their own daughter. When I told them that their son and I decided not to be married his mom was shocked and disappointed for a while.

Later, Godot became in charge of a financial leasing company in Shanghai. He asked me to work on a highway development project for him and offered me a nice apartment by the Huang Pu River in Pudong, Shanghai. I agreed, because I found a very good English school, Wall Street English Institution, nearby his office building.

The project company was called Shanghai Ze Feng Asset Management Company, and it was owned by two people, Clever and Jade. Clever was Godot's former boss at the bank, Jade was a former bank teller and born in the tiger year of 1962. I was impressed that all tiger women I knew were very beautiful and Jade was not an exception. So, I secretly called her Tiger Woman to my friends.

THE TIGER WOMAN PULLS THE TIGER'S SKIN, CASE III

Later, I found out that Shanghai Ze Feng Asset Management Company had no money but millions of dollars of debt. They borrowed money to invest and all their investments failed. However at this time, the Tiger Woman managed to get a chance to build a 11.3 billion yuan (about $1.4 billion dollars then) worth of a highway, because she knew the chief of Hangzhou Highway Bureau and the CFO of a government owned company, SIIC. She also knew a retired army official who served as one of the 9 standing members of politburo in the central government.

For many years, my business had been selling something or producing something to make money, I could never imagine one can make money from nothing. There is a Chinese idiom says that, no matter how smart a wife is, she can not make rice without rice. Well, this highway project was an eyeopening experience for me: to learn how to make rice *without* rice.

In fact, it was a game of borrowing a hen to lay eggs. First, the Tiger Woman asked the chief of the Hangzhou Highway Bureau to allow her company to invest in the Hang-Qian Highway. Such business usually would not be given to a company like Shanghai Ze Feng, because it had nothing but debt. However, it made a difference when the beautiful Tiger Woman invited Dr. Wu, the younger brother of the top official to become Chairman of her Board. Yes, in China, we call this "pulling the tiger's skin". This was a game similar to Madam Zhang Yu Fei planting the tree in Guang Dong.

With Dr. Wu as her honored Chairman of the Board, the Tiger Woman could easily borrow 200 million yuan (about $25 million dollars then) from SIIC, owned by the government with deep pockets. Thus, Shanghai Ze Feng Asset Management Company (SZFAMC) became one of the three shareholders of the Hang-Qian highway.

Not only that, the Tiger Woman signed a contract with SIIC by which it agreed to sell its all shares in the highway project to her company, in two years, at the original share price. This meant two years later her company would end up with 2/3 of the project. The projected budget for this highway was 6.5 billion yuan (about $800 million dollars then), but it ended up costing 11.3 billion yuan (about $1.4 billion dollars then).

Dr. Wu looked exactly like his elder brother. One may easily mistake him as his elder brother, since his brother has been on the news frequently. At the signing ceremony banquet, Dr. Wu made a toast to the table of government officials: "Hey, brothers and sisters, be careful, don't be caught!" to loud cheers.

During the breakfast the next day, Dr. Wu said that he was just a doctor, and knew nothing about business. This honored chairman of the board of a real estate company in Shanghai asked us what a mortgage might be. After he left, we took his wife to spend several days on Thousand Island Lake where the highway would go.

The town of Thousand Island Lake was very clean and beautiful. We spent several days with Dr. Wu's wife at Shanghai Ze Feng's beautiful and huge property in Thousand Island Lake, and we chatted almost everything. She told me that her husband was also on the board of their friend's real estate company, and their son was an investment banker. She said, "we only help the companies that have real substance, 'we won't throw out food without seeing the rabbit.'"

During the dinner hosted by the mayor Huang of Thousand Island Lake, I heard that Shanghai Ze Feng did not pay the payment required for purchase of the land. The Tiger Woman told mayor Huang, that when the highway project started, they would be able to pay then. See, she even knew how to lay eggs before the hen was borrowed.

I left Shanghai before the project finished, so I don't know the details about who made how much, heard from Godot that the cost had almost doubled at the end. He cautioned me not to assume there was any corruption in this deal.

So I asked him, "what the compensation was for Dr. Wu to be the honored chairman of Shanghai Ze Feng?"

"300 yuan/year (about $40 dollars/ year)."

"Do you believe that?"

He refused to respond.

Later when I mentioned this experience to a friend from the Treasury Department of the Central Government, he responded: "For each kilometer of highway in China, there is one communist party leader falls. There is a popular saying around, if all party members lined up, and you kill them all, there are people wronged. But if you kill every other one, there will be bad people who escape punishment." By this time, I thought that corruption was only a feature of authoritarian regimes, but later I realized that it's everywhere in human history, the US is no exception.

A BLUE EYED BEAR

THE BEAR EMERGES

Due to the pressure from my parents, I started a serious search for a potential life partner, but, with no luck. I met countless men, but nothing happened. So, I gave up and stopped paying for my match.com membership fees and the local matchmaker's service fees. However, I did not want to discourage my friend Susan, the former girlfriend of my client commander Huang, from doing so. I still helped her answer her emails every so often, because my English was better than hers.

One day, when I was living in Shanghai and logged into Susan's account on match.com to help her answering emails, a new subscriber's ad caught my eyes. He had no picture in his profile, just said he was 43 and looking for a willowy woman cuddling a bear. I thought that was a depiction of me, because I loved fussy bear toys. So, I sent this guy a message from Susan's account, "You sound as though you are looking for me."

He answered back instantly and left his name, Bill. He was very funny although I forgot what he exactly said in that email. So I told him that I was not Susan but Susan's friend, and asked him to exchange a picture. He liked my picture that showed only my hand and sent me back one that only showed his beautiful blue eyes.

We both were intrigued and started to chat through AOL's instant messenger. Since we both were busy, the communications were not deep during the first few weeks. We did not even tell each other what we did for a living, he once thought I was a farmer, because when he asked me what I was doing from the instant messenger, I typed: "working on my rice and carrots." I just wanted to tell him that I was working on nothing special.

I gradually grew to love the communication with Bill the Bear, because it was so different with all the other men I met. The other men were so material, or only paid attention to my looks, but the Bear, cared about my mind, soul, health and emotions: he was very funny. The other men bought me material goods to please me, but the Bear sent me books to feed my spirit, and food to nurture my body; he even mailed me beets and corn bread that he made for me from scratch. I was very touched and caught up by my discussions with him. We became emotionally involved very fast. I was amazed how a virtual relationship could be developed through thin air.

The Bear called me on phone every day to discuss the books or articles he sent me to read. The first book was fiction, *The Girl Who Played Go,* by Shan Sa and is a cross-cultural love story. It concerns a teenage Chinese girl who loved play I-go, a chess game with which I was always fascinated; she had no rival at her age until she met a stranger who was from Japan, the invader's country. It became a tragedy that could touch everyone's soul. The Bear also sent me another Anti-Japanese War related book, *Fragrant Harbor,* well written by John Lanchester. My English was improved after finishing both these books.

Although he disliked Hillary R. Clinton very much, the Bear sent me the autobiographies of the Clinton couple on my request. I told him that my Mom loved the Clintons very much, and I thought they were so charming and romantic. He didn't change his opinion but believed that I had the right to read what I wanted. I thought that was charming.

Then, we planned to meet in person after four months of cyber communication. The Bear let me choose from Hawaii, Thailand and The Phillipines. I had been to these two Asian countries, so I chose Hawaii.

When I landed in Hawaii Airport, the Bear was there, jumping like a kid, a big smile was on his face and his voice was metalic. We were so happy that we finally met in person, then he and I took another airplane flew to Maui. On this airplane, he told me that the wings of the plane were designed by his mother who was a successful aero physicist in Los Angeles where the McDouglas Airplanes made. He also told me that his mother was sent to China for an exchange program under President Nixon soon after Nixon shook Chairman Mao's hand. He was so proud of his mother Doris and I understood why, because I grew to be her fan too after I met her.

After we landed Maui Airport, the Bear rented a car and drove us to the Ritz Carlton Hotel by the beach. When we were reaching the hotel, I was excited and unconsciously started to sing the communist anthem, *International*. I told him that I was a communist coming here to reform him. He thought it was a joke because he would never believe a sophisticated woman like me could be a communist.

So, he asked me a lot of questions about politics in China in the first three days.
"How is the communist party doing in China?"
"They have been doing a great job!" I proudly responded.

Many years later, the Bear told me that, when he heard my response, his first impression was, "this girl is brainwashed." Then, after many years of our discussions, he realized that I was telling the truth, although I was also brainwashed.

For dinner at our first night, I dressed in a black Chinese Qi Pao with a soft orange color silk shawl. He looked at me as though I were a princess, and could not believe that this woman was a communist. I grew up with the party ideaology and never doubted its validity. Before I received my American education, I believed that communism was good for the poor and the capitalism only good for the rich. The Chinese people of my generation firmly believed the fallacies that a capitalist system only serves the rich, and a socialist system, which is a less advanced stage of a communism, serves the poor better than a capitalist system.

THE BEAR PROPOSES

The Bear gave me his arm and led me to the restaurant. We expressed our passionate feelings. Then, the Bear showed me a black and white movie, *Breakfast at Tiffany's*. After the movie ended, the Bear knelt down in front of me and proposed to me with a blue Tiffany & Co.'s box.

I was surprised, because we had only met in person for less than one day, and he was so courageous to take this risk. So, I said yes right away and warned him NOT to regret. I strongly felt that we both had the same character, typical of romantic risk taker's behavior. I loved this Bear and was glad I found him.

Maui was such a beautiful place and had many tropical plants that I had never seen before. We had a wonderful time there for a week. Then, my Chinese diet caused me trouble. I had to have rice every day but went without it for a week. So, my stomach got sick. The Bear was worried and asked the cook to make me a plate of fried rice. Since it was not on the menu, the hotel charged us $60 for it. I thought that was ridiculous, because it might cost just $6 dollars in a hotel in China. The Bear asked me to relax and not to worry about the price. So, I ate with deep guilty feelings. Since then, I knew my Bear truly loved me.

Later, he took me to the Chanel store to try clothes. I looked at the prices, refused to let him buy me anything from that store. I love beautiful things, but I don't have to own them.

Despite full of joys from falling in love, I could still sense the Bear's sorrow from his locked eyebrows. So, I asked him what caused it. This question opened the gate of a dam that had blocked the Bear's memory: how he was incredibly wronged by the Californian Attorney General, Bill Lockyer.

He spent several days to tell me his life stories, mostly very interesting and exciting, such as how he helped the former TV drama producer of *Dallas*, Aaron Spelling, to get his maid, who was an illegal immigrant, a passport. He actualy wrote an amazing fictional account of this, *The Saga of Nelia Doe,* based on his true experiences. However, the Lockyer persecution that was still unraveling was mind blowing. I could not believe that such injustice could happen in the USA, but it did.

THE TRAGEDY OF THE BEAR

On June 4th, 2002, the Bear's house and office were illegally raided by the police under the false charge that he and his partner stole money from a non-profit Children's Theatre they were building in Danvile, California. The informant, Sidney Corrie, was a "dear friend" of the attorney general, Bill Lockier. In 2005, the court concluded that the Bear did not steal money from his non-profit project, although Lockier's deputies swore to totally destroy the Bear with using taxpayer's dollars.

A week before I moved to Wellesley, MA, in 2009, the Bear received a box from the deputy attorney general's office of California. It was a box of all the documents about his case. The Bear requested it according to the Freedom of Information Act.

I picked up two documents to read. The first one was a letter drafted by Sidney Corrie[39]'s attorney, Putterman, on behalf of Corrie. The letter accused the Bear stealing money from his non-profit theater project, and asked Corrie's dear friend, the attorney general, Bill Lockyer, to indict the Bear.

---

[39] Sidney Corrie sold a piece of land to the Bear's company in 1997. To avoid taxes, he requested the Bear to inflate the agreed upon market price to pretend he donated a portion of his land to the non-profit theatre company. He then regretted the deal after he saw the land price increase. So, he colluded with his dear friend, Bill Lockier, the AG of California, to try to recover his land in a sham civil lawsuit. Corrie lost the civil lawsuit, then he asked Lockier to indict the Bear and his partner, and illegally raided the Bear's house and office to destroy his reputation. This was of course picked up by the press and destroyed the Bear's reputation in one headline.

A BLUE EYED BEAR 181

The second document was a draft of an agreement between the attorney general and Putterman regarding their willingness to share all the information about the Bear that both parties collected. So, it wasn't enough that the attorney general illegally raided the Bear's office on a false search warrant. What gave the AG the power to let a private law firm bringing a *civil* lawsuit take advantage of the information collected with taxpayers' money for a *criminal* lawsuit? If there were a law sanctioning this, then the law must be flawed.

After reading these two documents, I realized that I was wrong to doubt the Bear's innocence in the past, because I thought his allegation of State/private collusion was only an assumption. I wonder whether the judges had read those papers before they made their conclusions[40].

I felt sorry having doubted the Bear in the past as his spouse. I swore to myself that I would learn to write better English and tell this story to the Americans to initiate change. I would help raise fund to finish the Children's Theater[41] to prove the goodwill of the Bear and fulfill the generosity of the donators. That valuable asset should not be wasted, such a spirit of philanthropy should not be discouraged. And, the Californian people deserve to have a clean and efficient government. If we know something is wrong and not try to make a difference, we desert democracy and

---

[40] The court forced the Bear to give the unfinished non-profit Children's Theatre to Sidny Corrie, because otherwise, the attorney general Bill Lockier wouldn't unfreeze a bank account that held almost $4 million dollars which were supposed to pay back the bank loan.

[41] The Children's Theatre project had to be aborted though it was almost finished, due to the intervention from Bill Lockier.

Pictures of the Abandoned Children's Theater in Danville, CA

Pictures of the Abandoned Children's Theater in Danville, CA

ensure our eventual enslavement.

The Bear's life stories made me admire him more, because I tend to be attracted to troubled people. Their lives usually are more interesting and exciting than the lives of ordinary people who do not like initiate changes or confront challenges. However, my life's exciting path was also difficult, as it would appear I had to be constantly tested.

THE BEAR CAVES

THE BEAR'S ADVENTURE IN EASTERN CHINA

After we departed Hawaii, we missed each other so much. So, in September 2003, the Bear went to China to see me and we toured Shanghai, Suzhou, Hangzhou, Xiamen, Shenzhen and Hong Kong together for two weeks. The Bear also brought the son of his client, Steve Patmont, Tim Patmont, to see whether there was any expansion opportunity for their famous Goped motor scooter business.

Tim was in his mid 20's and never been to China. I had learned one English word from him and that was "bizarre," because he used it to express his feelings whenever he saw something that was unique to him. He was impressed by the fastest magnetic train in the world, and many other advanced technologies being used everywhere he went. Huge construction machines and cranes were operating everywhere as far as the eye could see.

The Bear enjoyed almost everything in China. Although he expressed that he woundn't eat snakes, dogs, cats, etc., I still threatened to feed him snake without telling him. One time, I gave him something to try and asked him how he liked it. He said it tasted great and he knew what it was. He believed that was bean curd, but in fact, it was the goat brain; once discovered, this sent him running to the loo.

He once ate something and said to me, "the noodles taste great."

"Hey, these arenot noodles, they are something from a *duck*."

"WHAT?"

Since my English wasn't clear, and he thought it was part of a *dog*, his face turned red and his eyebrows raised.

Besides enjoying wonderful and diverse food, this trip was also fruitful for business, if the owner of Goped then had a cristal ball. Our Xiamen visit revealed that at least one Chinese manufacturer was producing fake Goped scooters and shipping them to the U.S. market. We visited Suzhou Industrial Park and Shanghai Congming Island as sites for a potential Goped factory location. Each of the local governments welcomed us and introduced preferential policies for foreign investments.

These investigations revealed:

1) That Goped's market dominance had been stolen and immediate action was needed to protect it;

2) The Chinese government created smart policies to attract foreign investments.

What was the US doing at that time? Invading Iraq and promoting Globalization, at the cost of the American people's economic sovereignty and liberty. Yes, liberty! If your resources are taken away by the government, you can't grow, you can't travel, although the US Constitution promises your natural right to pursue happiness and prosperity.

THE BEAR'S FIRST CAVE

Before the trip finished, I brought the Bear to meet Godot's parents, and they liked each other. Then, I followed the Bear back to a beautiful place called Genoa, Nevada where the Bear owned a new house. I fell in love with it immediately.

The Bear was still separated from his wife Deb, who was living in their old house in Danville, CA. Later I met Deb frequently at family reuninions and came to know she is a great woman. I could not understand why their long marriage could not withstand challenges, since they both were such good people.

After I stayed in Nevada for about one month, my best friend Jasmine joined me. She spent one day with us and came to the conclusion that I should marry the Bear. Her reasoning:
"He is not like some other Americans who are not flexible." Yes, many immigrants believe that the Americans are inflexible in general.

Then the Bear took us to Los Angeles where we met his parents. His stepfather Steward and mother Doris were retired engineers. Steward told us that he had worked for Peiking Duck while studying in Stanford. Doris was an extremely beautiful and elegant elderly woman who looked much younger than her age. She wore a white linen shirt with a silver rose pin on her left chest. She had given her blue eyes to the Bear, so beautiful and clear. Jasmine said that Doris was a real noble woman with both beauty and brains. I fell in love with her immediately.

As we have seen, Doris had been to China for a cultural exchange program during Nixon's presidency. She told me that Beijing University's library must still have her book on aeronautics. She even had a huge black and white photo of her with the Great Wall behind.

Doris and her husband Steward were also philanthropists who actively participated in community charity events. They advocated for the Homeless Children of Los Angeles County, and found foster homes for them. She was also a member of the Board of Directors of a branch of the Los Angeles symphony orchestra, and, a donor to the Walt Disney Center for the Arts in downtown Los Angeles.

The Bear and I were once invited to the Disney Center for a fundraising event, which raised money from their neighborhood friends to allow foster kids to go to college. When we were looking for our seats, the Bear pointed out a seat that has Doris' name engraved on it for her contribution. I realized that charitable spirit had been in the Bear's family tradition for generations. Probably, his grandparents brought it from Ireland.

However, Doris sounded not so much in love with China as the Bear. She said that she did not like the people who forced her to drink Mao Tai,[42] and watch the Peking Opera when all she wanted to do was washing her hair. Well, *that* was one example of a cultural gap.

Another example of cultural gap was, when Doris asked my opinion about something, I would answer her:

"We think…"

She stared at me, "who are '*we*'?"

Instead of understanding her confusions, I felt offended. I thought,

"Don't all Chinese think the same, since we read the same books and watched the same TV programs?"

---

[42] The best Chinese alcohol.

Yes, the Chinese media speaks with one voice. We believed one voice was better than many, especially when the country had appeared to turn in the right direction from the wrong. After decades of Chaos, we believe stability is the foundation of everything, and 'development is the absolute principle[43].' Doesn't it align with the spirit of the US Constitution?

Mama Doris in her 40's By Jin Lan

---

[43] This theory came from Deng Xiao Ping.

As a result of years of brainwashing, most Chinese people, including myself, got used to believing whatever the government media told us. So, I did not even notice that my tone of voice was exactly the same as that of a CCTV[44] announcer. I had become used to use the word "we" to express my opinion, because I believed we all should think the same, since key words, such as "all the people with one mind", were engraved in every Chinese subconscious since birth. I felt unpatriotic if I didn't think the same.

THE BEAR'S CAVE IN THE BOHEMIAN GROVE

Later, the Bear took Jasmine and I to the Redwoods above the bay area where the Bohemian Grove is located. The natural beauty of the grove was breathtaking, hundreds of camps spread out along the length of a beautiful valley with ancient redwoods at its base. We had fun with the Bear's friends, but unfortunately, the poor English of Jasmine and me prevented us from knowing what his friends were saying, and we could not understand the various cultural events going on there.
Before we left, the Bear asked me, "How do you feel about this place?"
"The place is beautiful, but why all the people are old? Where are the younger people?"
"It's a special group of people selected from a waiting list where a man might wait for decades to become a member."
"Really?"

---

[44] The TV station owned by the central government of China.

I still had no idea what that meant until later when I read some anti-American allegations on Chinese media. Some people believed that it was not the US government that ran the United States, but the special men's clubs, such as the Bohemian Club and the Bilderberg Group. It is also believed that these groups run all the governments in the world, because their all male members are the elite of the elite. I don't know how true that statement is, because from what I have seen the members of the club are there to enjoy music, art and literature.

One of my favorite activities there were the club's Spring & Fall Picnics, because those were outdoor activities to which the members could bring their ladies and friends. These activities give them an opportunity to see and walk in the grove. There were different programs at different locations, and each camp also had its own party going on. One may choose to listen to a lakeside lecture by a scientist like Dr. Filipenko or a politician like Collin Powell or attend a piano solo by a Grammy winner, or take in combination of even more electic shows.

My favorite is always the magic shows. One time, the magician Patrick Martin asked a guy from the audiences to help him on the stage, when the guy got on the stage, Patrick asked him, "What's your name?"

"Henry."

"Henry, can you show me your wallet?"

Henry took out his wallet.

"Can you give me one note?"

"No."

So Patrick grabbed Henry's wallet and took one note from it, then tore it into two pieces. Henry asked him to give back. Patrick only gave him a half and the other half was thrown into a large yellow box, where it disappeared.

Henry kept asking Patrick for the other half of the note. Patrick get his hand into the yellow box and retrieved a yellow lemon.

Henry, "I don't want a lemon, I want my money back."

Patrick took out a knife and split the lemon. Inside was the other half of the note!

So, Henry got excited, "More yellow, please!"

Then, Patrick extracked a bunch of lemons from the box and threw them into the audiences. Eventually, the last yellow thing that came out from the box was a man in a girl's dress[45]. This man was Michael Ganz, the Bear's old friend who was a psychiatrist. In fact, the 'Henry' was Dr. Henry Kissinger who was well known in China since when I was a child. I saw his black and white picture with Chairman Mao in the newspaper, but never thought that I would see him in person or be invited to his office.

However, for the Bear, his favorite things were music and poetry. He played his banjo and ukulele whenever he got a chance and read his poetry to people to cheer their spirit. He was a great writer, especially his poetry. He wrote articles and poems for the Club's magazine frequently. In fact, he was invited to be a Bohemian member because of his special talent in poetry, at a time when he was studying to be a lawyer.

---

[45] All the roles of women in their shows must be acted by men, because the Bohemian Club has no female members.

One day, during the summer break when he was a law school student, he had to make some money to pay for his groceries. So, he walked into a law office building in San Francisco, tried to find a summer job. People there asked him what he could do, he answered he could do anything, from washing dishes to writing poems. Then he recited a poem written by himself when he was age 18:

A Tragedy in Lower Mechanics

*By lesbos' fair shores, where the Nereids play,
in profligate sin lived a Volkswagen gray.*

*His pistons were ruptured, the tires were shot,
he ran, not on gas, but on liquefied pot.*

*Both bumpers were pitted and covered with rust,
the product, no doubt, of insatiable lust.*

*A passion which triggered all that Volks did,
merely to sate a libidinous id.*

*Down by the sea ran a boulevard dark,
where autos in love were accustomed to park.*

*And here on a Saturday night re repaired,
"Out with the boys", the excuse his wife heard.*

*Hard by a ditch lay his atrophied bod,
faint with the hopes of making some broad.*

*When what to his lecherous eyes should appear,
but a black XK-E, with a Plexiglas rear.*

*His engine set racing, both lights gone a flame,
his clutch disengaged at the sigh of the dame.*

*For as well as her torque and cubic addition,
the beetle was turned on by no mere ignition.*

*He always had craved to make love to a chick,
running a hydro instead of a stick.*

*The Jag swiveled with grace her rear end of
plexy, giving the Volks a look oh-so-sexy.*

*Till his shabby condition, hidden by night,
was revealed in the dazzling glare of her lights.*

*Then she escaped with a deafening screech,
choosing a road adjacent to the beach.*

*Scared by his visage and loathful to neck,
or anything else, with the impotent wreck.*

*But quite unabashed by this slap in the face,
Volksie decided to give her a chase.*

*And sealing his fate, with his wiper blades crossed,
he followed the scent of her perfumed exhaust.*

Through hair pin and spiral they quickened their speed,
  dangerous play for cars gone to seed.

  For a bend in the road held the Jag in its trap,
  and in a matter of moments, the romance was scrap.

  So, now they are in Pluto yet able to brag,
  of roding far hotter than Jupiter's drag.

  For once everyday, with the aid of jack,
  the Volkswagen is carted away to a track.

  Where he chases for miles, but never gets near,
  that black XK-E, and her Plexiglas rear.

People in the office loved his poem, so they hired him to fetch ice for their afternoon cocktail party. Among them there was a gentleman, Sidney Lawrence, who appreciated the Bear's talent so much he voluntarily sponsored the Bear to be a candidate of the Bohemian club and put him on the waiting list. In 1989, the Bear became a formal member of the club and started to have fun with his new friends.

INSPIRED BY THE BEAR

The Bear's creative mind constantly generating new ideas. I had been inspired by him frequently since I met him. He once helped me to improve my first English poem.

Genoa's Veil

Genoa's winter is as a shy bride,
So intrigued, I would offer her a ride,
But where can I elope with her to,
Since she is from the heavens and
Can disappear like a drop of morning dew?

I could not find the proper words to end the poem, it took him only one second to use the translation of my Chinese name to form a perfect ending. The Bear gave me countless inspiration for the rest of my life, and he felt the same coming from me.

The Bear has a lot of friends, and I met many of them. They all said that he had changed quite a bit since he met me, from an angry man to a happy Bear. They knew of the Bear's war with Bill Lockyer[46], but still trusted his integrity. I grew to love the Bear more and more each day and inspired my second English poem:

If...

If you were the mountain
I'd like to be the river
Gently embrace you
With my endless love

If you were the river

---

[46] This amazing story is written in a book called, *Children's Theater*, by Jin Lan McCann. Coming out soon!

I'd like to be the mountain
Let you lie down in my warm arms
But still allow you to freely flow
To anywhere you want to be

If you were the wind
I'd like to be the sand
And joyfully follow you
To wherever you blow me to

If you were the blue sky
I'd like to be the white cloud
Decorate your magnificent life
With my most creative art of nature

If you were the piano
I'd like to be the pianist
Passionately play for you
The most romantic notes of my life

If you were the lighted candle
I'd like to be the humble moth
Show you my last beautiful dance
With my life disappearing in your fire

In the fall of 2004, the Bear and I got married on the Mid-Autumn's Festival Day in my hometown Chongqing. The Bear had great fun with my high school classmates at the wedding. I could not believe they had been talking to each other all night in different languages, not understanding each other, and yet no one got bored.

None of the classmates could speak English, and the Bear could only remember a few animal names in Mandarin, such as, "Xiong Mao" for panda, and "Qing Wa" for frog. He had fun with the word "Qing Wa", because it was pronounced the same as the name of China's best university, Qing Hua. He could not distinguish 'Hua' and 'Wa'.

Then One day, we went to a paddlefish restaurant and he learned its Mandarin name, "Ya Zui Yu". When he saw a fish with a duck mouth, he knew that was an almost extinct species from the Mississippi river and was surprised that the Chinese people ate them. We had great fun dipping this fish in hotpot and I wrote a poem about the Paddle fish:

The Saga of the A Paddlefish

-For Shenzhen Paddlefish Restaurant

One day, my mom was playing around,
In the Mississippi where no one could be found.
Someone with a duck mouth complimented her,
'Such a wonderful blond!'
And wanted to take her to a beautiful wonder pond.

My mom was so madly in love,
She did not think it through,
Just followed him to a pool with a boat above
They sailed all the way to China,
Where everyone had no entertainment,
Except making babies for fun.

Here, they made lots of us,

With long duck mouths like my dad's.
Now, we are so cool and precious,
People want us and cook us in their hot pots.

People praised me a lot,
Because I am so goddamn hot!
Sorry, now I must say goodbye,
For humans who say they would protect me,
Lie!

I never could imagine, some day, I might write poems in another language. They just flowed like a fountain after this talent was discovered by the Bear. Yes, the Bear helped me discover many potential skills I never know. He might have been an angel sent by God to inspire me.

After we got married, the Bear return to the States. To protect me, he had me stay in China, but occasionally I flew to the US to see him. In May 2005, he was convicted a felony by contra Costa County Superior Court, for allegedly filing a false state tax return eight years before, and was sentenced to 180 days in jail with five years probation. In addition, he lost his law license in California and had to take another bar exam to get a Nevada law license, which he did.

However, the Bear was released after two weeks, because the sheriffs had never heard of anyone imprisoned for allegedly filing a false state tax return in 1997 and convicted 8 years later. The Bear, of course, still did not believe that he had done anything illegal, but no one in the court would believe him, or do their own investigation, and relied on the attorney general's twisted reports[47]. I could not believe the Bear could be so wronged, but I found ample evidence to prove it seven years later.

ADVENTURE IN IRELAND

The Bear later went to the National University of Ireland to get his masters' degree in creative writing. I joined him in Ireland to support his continue education in 2006. Over there, Mona Lisa smiled at me and told me, "you should go to Wellesley College." Well, where is it?

I was fascinated by the Irish sense of humor from the first day I landed Dublin. When we were riding in a cab and I asked the taxi driver whether Irish men drink a lot, he answered me, "noooooooooo, we don't drink a lot, at all."
"Really?"
"We only drink an *awful* lot."

Then, I saw a bar near the court house. The name of the bar was "The Deaf Judge". I guess the owner understood the feelings of people who lose in court and provided a place for them to release their anger.

In Galway, we had the chance to celebrate the Cuirt Literature Festival with the Nobel laureate poet Seamus Heaney, and some other western poets. Each of them recited their own poems, which inspired me greatly. I never realized that I could write poems and paint like a natural, but I can,

---

[47] Seven years later, I read the court records and found out that many statements made by the attorney general and the court were untrue. Although those misstatements did not directly affect the sentence, they damaged the Bear's credibility and the chance he deserved to correct his past mistake made 8 years ago.

now. I didnot have my own poem then, so I recited an ancient poem by Li Bai, from the Tang Dynasty. The audience was fascinated.

During our time in Ireland, my ex-boyfriend Godot sent me numerous documents about Clean Development Mechanism programs and wanted me to study about it. I was close-minded and would not read thick documents that were technically difficult. So, I fought with Godot when we were talking on phone.

The Bear heard this dispute and said,
"Please don't be rude to Godot, he is such a sweetheart."
"He let me do something that I don't understand and have no idea how to do it."
"What does he want you to do?"
"He wants me to be involved with a CDM[48] business that I have no knowledge about."
"I know about this business, let him send the documents to me."

After the Bear studied those documents, he told me that Godot was doing a great thing for China and I should be proud of him. Then, the Bear explained what the Kyoto Protocol was, and all the related terminology. So I started to understand how this enterprise could benefit both investors and fight global warming, by promoting green energy projects with new and efficient technologies.

While studying about this business, I found out that the environmental situation in China was much worse than I knew. The good news is that we could make a difference to it if we act before it was too late. I told the Bear that I would

---

[48] Clean Development Mechanism

learn better English and do something positive and meaningful for China. He supported this idea and said that he would back me. Then the Bear and Godot decided to became partners in a clean development project, and I became their coordinator.

With Nobel Laureate Poet Seamus Heaney & Other Western Poets at Curt Literature Festival

Before we left Ireland, I rented a fascinating movie, *Mona Lisa Smile*. It was a story about an inspirational female art history professor at Wellesley College in the 1960's. After watching it, I told the Bear, "I want to study at this school."

"Of course, you can!"

This was why I loved the bear. He would never step on my dreams, even when he believed it was impossible. One year later, when I received a rejection letter from Wellesley College, he told me that he hadnot wanted to discourage me when I told him I wished to go to Wellesley. He knew it was impossible since his daughters, who were so brilliant, would not be able to get in. He told me this to comfort my wounded soul, but I had become determined to go to Wellesley College.

COULD THE 2008 DEBACLE HAVE BEEN AVOIDED?

After we returned from Ireland, I applied to Wellesley College and was rejected. So I enrolled in Western Nevada College, a very nice school near our home in Genoa, Nevada. The school gave me a placement test for English and maths, before enrollment. When I walked out of the test room, I saw the Bear's face covered with tears.
"Why tears, Bear?"
"I am so proud of you! Your math score is 20 points more than the school's record, although English is new to you."
"I told you I was good at mathematics, why are you still surprised?"
"I knew you were good, but I did not know you were *that* good." Well, it might be special for a left-handed Bear who was math challenged, not for a Chinese woman raised by a tiger Mom.

WHO ATE BEAR STEARNS?

I had been receiving straight A grades at the school while I was assisting and coordinating the Carbon Trade business for Godot and the Bear, so he never had to worry about my studies. During the summer of 2007, the Asset Research Center of the Central Government of China invited us and the Bear's jointventure partner, Cantor Fitzgerald, to a forum in Beijing. This forum also invited bankers from various countries. So, I had the chance to sit with Ms. Liu, who was the president of a branch of CITIC group, at the banquet. Although I did not pay much attention to this new contact, the Bear did.

After we returned to the USA in the fall, the Bear asked me to introduce the head of CITIC to a client of his friend's son in New York City. This relationship sounded difficult to arrange. I just had a dinner with Ms. Liu and had no idea whether she had a good relationship with her big boss, or not. I wasn't sure I could help, so I ignored the Bear's request for a while. Then the Bear kept insisting/; "The Yang[49], Michael truly needs your help, please help him."

So, he forwarded relevant emails to me. I learned what the New York client desired. Whether there was anything that CITIC could do about it, or might be interested, was another question.

After reading through the emails, I realized that the New York client was Alfonse Fletcher, the founder and CEO of a hedge fund that was trying to purchase $3 billion dollar's worth of convertible notes of Bear Stearns[50]. By then, Bear Stearns' stock price had fallen to around $40 from $133 in less than one year. However, strangely, Mr. Fletcher did not want to use his own firm's name to buy these convertible notes. Instead, he wanted to use CITIC's name to hold the investment through a Sino-American joint venture. This might give the market the impression that Chinese deep pockets were preparing to take over Bear Stearns. Using a

---

[49] Yang is a lamb in Chinese, the Bear calls me Yang, because I was born in the year of lamb in Chinese lunar calendar.

[50] Of course, at the time, I did not know that Bear Stearns had a liquidity problem.

company not his own for this transaction might also have been inspired by worries about racial discrimination, since he is an African American.

I asked Godot whether he could connect Mr. Fletcher with the head of CITIC. He consulted his friend. Then we were told that CITIC would be interested in this deal only if Mr. Fletcher would also use this joint venture to invest in Carbon Trade businesses. After passing this information to Mr. Fletcher, he agreed to dedicate a portion of the joint venture to do Carbon Trade business, but insisted on managing the rest of the operation.

To accelerate this deal, Mr. Fletcher proposed that CITIC did not need to put cash into the joint venture, only its name. However, CITIC would not take advantage from him and would put cash into the deal equal to its portion of ownership. In October, both sides expressed their sincere intention of forming a partnership. Then Mr. Fletcher and the Bear flew to Beijing to meet with David, the vice president of CITIC group, in December 2nd, 2007.

Mr. Fletcher told the Bear that he worked for Bear Stearns after graduated from Harvard. He believed that Bear Stearns had treated him well, so when Bear Stearns had trouble with liquidity, he wanted to help. Of course, though he said he was trying to help, I believe his real intention was to take over control of Bear Stearns.

The Bear trusted Mr. Fletcher's good intentions and tried his best to convince David, the CEO of CITIC, that this deal would benefit both China and America. David accepted the Bear's proposal since it had a Carbon Trade component in the joint venture[51]. After Mr. Fletcher and the Bear returned to the USA from Beijing, they worked out a MOU and David presented it at the board meeting and it passed in short order, unusual speed for such a huge enterprise.

Although the board of CITIC group approved the joint venture, the story did not have a happy ending. Though I did not know the reason at the time, Mr. Fletcher first arranged to visit Beijing to start the joint venture in the beginning of Jan, 2008; then he postponed the trip for 90 days; then he gave up the plan entirely. So, what transpired during the 90 days?

According to Wikipedia, "On March 14th, the Federal Reserve Bank of New York agreed to provide a $25 billion loan to Bear Stearns collateralized by free and clear assets from Bear Stearns in order to provide Bear Stearns the liquidity for up to 28 days that the market was refusing to provide". However, the Fed changed its mind for some mysterious reasons in two days after this announcement. The NY Fed decided to support J.P. Morgan Chase with $29 billion dollar's loan backed by Bear Stearns' assets, and allow J.P. Morgan Chase to merge with Bear Stearns in a stock swap which unreasonably undervalued Bear Stearns share price at $2 per share.

After a fierce fight, Bear Stearns' shareholders eventually agreed to settle at $10 per share at the end of March 2008. This deal only cost J.P. Morgan Chase $1.2 billion dollars. I wondered why Mr. Fletcher's $3 billion dollar scheme

---

[51] In many occasions, Chinese government owned entities would do business for political purposes other than economic benefit. Carbon Trade business then was extremely risky since there was almost no market.

didnot obtain control of Bear Stearns, since he claimed he offered much more than $1.2 billion dollars before the stock price crashed.

He might have dreamed for years that he would one day take control of Bear Stearns. Did he lose confidence in Bear Stearns as the SEC Chairman Christopher Cox said, "Bear Stearns' problems escalated when rumors spread about its liquidity crisis which in turn eroded investor confidence in the firm although it still has high quality collateral to provide as security for borrowings." Was it true that investors like Mr. Fletcher lost confidence in Bear Stearns, or were the small fish chased by a predatory shark?

While studying economics at Wellesley College in 2011, enrolled in a macroeconomics seminar conducted by professor Daniel Sichel, who was a chief director of the senior economic consulting board for Ben Bernanke. In this seminar, we concluded that one of the triggers of the 2008 Recession was the collapse of Bear Stearns and Leman Brothers. They were forced to sell their assets at margin call due to overleverage. I wonder if Mr. Fletcher completed his $3 billion dollar purchase of the convertible notes before March 2008, and if the Fed's $25 billion in assistance been given at that time, would that have boosted investor confidence, saved Bear Stearns from selling assets at discounted prices, and in turn prevented failure of the whole financial market?

Whenever a murder happens a detective's first response is to identify who is the beneficiary of the death. In this case, the beneficiary of the death of Bear Stearns was J.P. Morgan Chase. Not only did it buy Bear Stearns at the lowest price, it received a $29 billion cheap loan from the

Fed, backed by Bear Stearns' assets, instead of J.P. Morgan Chase's own assets.

Of course, one may argue that Bear Stearns was not murdered, but committed suicide from over leveraging. However, why did the Fed, if it knew Bear Stearns was about to die and such death might cause chaos in the financial markets, withdraw its $25 billion dollar life saver? If one looks into the details and the players involved, one can answer that question.

When the NY Fed withdrew its promise to lend $25 billion dollars to help Bear Stearns in March 2008, who was on its board? Jamie Dimon, who was the chairman of the board of J.P. Morgan Chase, also served as a Class A director of the Board of Directors of the NY Fed. No wonder Bear Stearns was allowed to be eaten by a shark. Such is the rule of nature. Prior my class at Wellesley, I thought the United States had anti trust laws to prevent predators from damaing its economy.

The swallowing of Bear Stearns and Lehman Brothers by the big sharks didn't prevent the recession. Later that summer, when I took our friends from Stanford to travel all over China, they were amazed by its advancement, technology, and economic dynamism. This was in stark contrast to the gloomy US economy, the country's deteriorated infrastructure, and the desperate condition of working people in the US. Astounded at China's amazing achievements, our friends repeatedly said to me, "the Chinese government must have done something right!" I was so proud of my motherland, although I didn't know that the 'something right' had nothing to do with communist ideology, but with the adoption of Reagonomics, a process which began with the

Macroeconomic Summit on the cruiseship where I worked in 1985.

CUTTING THE DECK

Another eyeopening experience for me was the role of a deck of cards in the 2008 presidential election during the primary campaign, when Hillary R. Clinton and Barack Obama were the Democratic candidates. Although my Mom, Father and I had been in love with Hillary since she became First lady of the United States, the Bear never trusted her. I asked him multiple times why, but he did not offer meaningful answers until one day I raised this question again, because I thought his view unreasonable.
"There are plenty of reasons why I don't trust her. First, she is dangerous, second, she is an opportunist, instead of a sound politician like Lincoln, Kennedy or Reagan, who served with integrity."
The Bear then said:
"When she was young, she supported Barry Goldwater who was a Republican running for president, and who swore he would use nuclear weapons to bomb North Vietnam. Then, she became Democrat, but voted for the war in Iraq, which was a Republican strategy. The world would be a much safer place without her type of politicians, who don't study consequences before they vote. Really, I don't think she reads as extensively as did her husband or Lincoln.
"She probably just listened to her staff's summary of the documents concerning the justification for the War, and was influenced by filtered information. Or, if she did read them,

she could not understand them, and made a bad judgement. Maybe, she wanted to appear strong and not fearful of war, so voted for it no matter how flawed the reasoning, or how dire the consequences.

"In any event, I don't think she is ready to lead this country, which is in a serious trouble and needs leadership of intelligence and integrity. In addition, I don't think her political conversion was genuine, or from the heart. She likely converted for political opportunity."

Since I had limited knowledge about America, I offered no counter argument. He followed the 2008 campaign news and thought that Hillary was going to win the Democratic primary. He was upset and said that if Hillary won the presidency, he would immigrate to Thailand.

Then the news reported that there was a group called 'Republicans for Obama' in Nevada. For Republicans to support a Democratic candidate against their predicted strong rival was a clever strategy, because it gave the Republican candidate a better chance to win.

At the time, the Republicans thought that Hillary had more backers and would be a stronger rival than Barack Obama. The Bear thought this strategy sound. After several debates on TV, the Bear concluded that the one Democrat candidate who might be able to beat Hillary R. Clinton was Barack Obama.

The Bear read the books written by Obama and did thorough research about him. He felt that Obama was the right man for America, because he had shown sound judgement and was a peace lover throughout his life. The Bear joined Obama campaign, because he did not believe that any of the Republican candidates would make changes America needed at the time, and thought Obama was wiser than Hillary.

The Bear called the Obama Campaign Team and volunteered to help. The campaign manager appointed the Bear captain of our precinct, where most residents were conservatives. A high school boy was assigned to assist the Bear; we attended various campaign events in town and had conference calls with Barack Obama.

I was excited and engaged, because, in my life I had never participated a presidential campaign and was curious to learn how it worked. Many people in China believe that all American political campaigns are manipulated by the rich. I was interested to learn how the American people keep the elections honest, and how they identify proper candidates.

Before the Nevada Caucus, Barack Obama came to Carson City and gave a speech to the residents. It was an evening during the cold winter of 2007; nearly one thousand people lined up around Carson City Civic Center expecting to see and talk to Obama. Unfortunately, the Civic Center was not big enough for so many people, and we had to have the tickets to get in. Since the Bear was a precinct captain, he had a ticket, but I had to sneak in with a campaign manager's help.

After I entered the Civic Center, I noticed big media cameras on either side of the hall. It took hours for everyone to be checked by security. Two of Obama's secret service men with ear plugs stood by the stage. Passionate young volunteers also stood on the stage behind the podium.

They frequently shouted "Obama for President, yes, we can..." to boost spirit. The audience responded with whistlng and waving posters. I settled next to a video camera that had a good view of the stage.

The local Democratic leader introduced Obama. Thirty minutes after his scheduled appearance, he came in and apologized to everyone for his being late, because he had to shake hands with more than three hundred people who could not attain admission and who waited outside to see him.

People cheered, and he gave a speech. After his speech, it was the Q & A time; he tried to convince the skeptics to support him; then a high school boy by my side grabbed the microphone. Obama saw him standing in the volunteer section and said: "You can not take the microphone, because you are a volunteer, please give the microphone to someone who has doubts about me."
The boy exclaimed to Obama: "but I Love You!"
Then he yielded the microphone to a grandmotherly lady in a wheelchair.
Obama then responded to the boy: "I Love You Back!"
I was so touched, because he was so sweet and sincere.

The lady in the wheelchair questioned Obama's electability because of his race. Several other skeptics also had the similar questions, because they did not want to select a Democrat candidate who could not win the general election. Obama acknowledged that there were biases against race and gender. Just as some people would not vote for him because he is black, there would be people who refused vote for Hillary because she is a woman, or people who would not vote for Edwards because they don't like his accent.
He raised the question,
"Can we get a majority of the American people to give us a fair hearing?" Obama showed by his Iowa victory that he

could get a fair hearing and receive victory in the final election.

The following week, we spent all our spare time knocking upon people's doors in several neighborhoods, inviting them to the Nevada Caucus. People in our town are very honest and respectful. If they had already decided to vote for someone else, they would tell us instead of being upset about our supporting a different candidate.

When the Bear asked some residents whether they believed that America was ready for a black man to lead the country, they all said yes. However, when the Bear asked whether they were ready to elect a woman to be the next president, some of the male residents were not ready, but all the female residents were. Although the outside weather was cold as we rambled through the neighborhoods, the excitement warmed my blood and I enjoyed the experience.

THE 2008 CAUCUS

The Caucus was in a primary school, ten minutes away from our home by car. On the Caucus Day, the Bear and I went there early to prepare. My job was directing the people to the right place.

The Bear kept calling people to come to vote for Obama. However, the captain of Hillary's team would not allow the Bear to enter the Caucus, because he was a registered Republican. So, the Bear registered as a Democrat right in front of her. Then, she let us in.

About fifteen minutes before the door closed, our group had only twelve people, while Hillary's supporting team had twenty-two. There were few people in Edwards' group. So, the Bear started to call our neighbors in the Genoa Lakes Golf Course subdivision. He knew that most of them were Republicans, but still asked them to be Democrats for just one day.

He might have made ten phone calls. Right before the door closed, four of our neighbors showed up and registered. Then the count started. On the first count, we had sixteen votes and Hillary had twenty-two votes. Then, each campaign captain was given five minutes to speak.

The captain of Hillary's supporting team was a very passionate lady, her face beet red when she stepped on a table to make her points. Then, the Bear got on another table and spoke to the crowd:

"I was a Kennedy supporter and a Reagan supporter, I have always supported what's good for America, with no political preference. This time, I support Barack Obama, because I believe history will prove him a great leader. His proposals are good for our future and for the world, and, they are practical, more likely to transire than Hillary's proposals. If we choose Obama as our President, the world will be a safer place, and he can make our lives better. And, he has outstanding intelligence and integrity, as evidenced by his personal history. His leadership would focus on what is good for the country, not what makes himself look good. He has a broad and substantive longterm view of our country and its place in the world."

I did not pay much attention to Edwards' group, because I did not think Edwards had a chance to win. After all the speeches finished, the participants started to realign. Our team absorbed some of Edwards supporters, so when the votes were tallied, we were tied with Hillary's team.

CUTTING THE DECK

However, there were only three delegate seats to be divided between our teams, so one of the seats was up for grabs. While I wondered how this would be decided, the chairman took out a deck of cards and asked the Bear and the captain of Hillary's team to each pick a card. The Bear picked a lower card than Hillary's captain, so she got to cut the deck. Then, each of them had to pick another card. This time, the Bear selected the Queen of Hearts, so our group won two of the three seats.

Later I learned that the Bear's efforts for Obama's Nevada Primary Campaign in 2008 had a more significant impact than I originally thought. Although Hillary won the popular vote, Barack Obama won thirteen delegates to Hillary's twelve. If the Bear had not been biased against Hillary, he would not have taken so much effort to study Obama and support him.

If we had not campaigned door to door, we might not have had twelve voters to start with. At the time Hillary had twenty-two votes to our twelve, if the Bear given up, he might not have called our neighbors to help in the last fifteen minutes. In fact, I could not believe our neighbors would show up on time, because they were known to be conservatives and the admission period was about to close.

If the Bear had not been so convining, our four neighbors might not have made the trip to be there on time. If the Bear's speech to the crowd did not score points, the people who were in Hillary's team might not have changed their minds. If the Bear did not have a good luck in drawing the cards, then, the winner of the Nevada Caucus wouldn't have been Barak Obama.

This was important, because Nevada was one of the earliest states to hold Caucus and its result might influence the decisions of people in other states. This amazing experience helped me to learn how democracy in action could be so effective by each of us just doing a little bit more. Or, we could contribute to the mistake of political apathy by not doing that little bit more.

Not long after the Caucus, the Bear's paralegal Deb died. It was a great loss for the Bear because he is a genuine, loving, and compassionate man. He cried quietly alone, and his eyes were red for days. While campaigning for Obama, he was in great pain. In 2008, we helped make history in America. I was glad that I could have the chance to observe how grassroots action may achieve greater success than the power of rich.[52]

However, years later, I realized that a party's success in a democratic election doesn't necessarily guarantee the country's success. It only avoids violent regime change, which is costly and destructive. I realized this fact after 10 years of extensive study of historical events, and some deep introspections.

---

[52] At that time, I did not know that grassroots movements could be manipulated by media controlled by 'pacs' or the super rich.

EMPOWERED BY WELLESLEY

ADMISSION TO WELLESLEY

In March 2009, I was admitted to Wellesley College as a Davis Scholar. I only got the admission email one midnight after I finished my homework. The Bear was asleep, so I did not wake him up.

When the Bear woke in the morning, I told him about the good news. He was happily surprised, because he did not even know that I applied to this school again, despite the fact that I was rejected before. He thought I had only applied to UC Berkeley since he helped me with that application.
"When did you know?"
"Last night."
"Why didn't you tell me last night?"
"You were sleeping, I did not want to wake you up."
"You should have woken me up, this is a great news."
"I thought I have to go Berkeley anyway, because it is closer to home. Isn't it our plan?"
"I am so proud of you! Who said that you can't go Wellesley? You are going there, because it is a better school for you than Berkeley. I am beginning to think that I am not good enough for you! Maybe I should give you away and let a Harvard man take care of you." He said this with tears streaming down his face.
"Don't worry, Bear, you are good enough for me."

I happily went to my local school and told my classmates and professors the good news. Almost everyone was happy for me, except for economics Professor David Brook who was a staunch conservative. Since I had been injected with communist ideology all my life, it was easy for me to adopt the liberal ideology and reject the conservative ideology. To me, communism and socialism represented fairness and caring, capitalism and conservatism represented selfishness and greed. So, I typically challenged Professor Brook's conservative views, and felt good when my classmates told me that they truly enjoyed my debate with him.

One time, Professor Brook drew on the board a box with four 'isms' on the corners: Fascism, Communism, Socialism and Capitalism. So, I asked him,
"In that box, which point is the most efficient?"
"I will let you find the answer."

The class laughed out loud. I guess he wanted us to conclude that capitalism is the most efficient. However, he hesitated to say so, because socialist China experienced two digital growth for decades, while the United States was heading into a great recession. I was so proud of the economic achievements of the Chinese Communist Party, despite rampant corruption throughout the society.

However, what I didn't know then was that it wasn't communist economic theory that helped China achieve its success, but Reaganomics. I later discovered that the major cause of the fall of the US Empire was its abandonment of Reaganomics while China and Russia consistently deregulated for decades. I will explain this in another chapter.

We took economics quizzes online every weekend, but sometimes, I believed that the standard answers were set up wrong and the computer graded us erroneously. Several times, I had to ask Professor Brook to correct my grades, so I had a chance to chat with him. From our conversations, I felt he thought I was the troublemaker in his class. One conversation went like this:

"You are a high performer in my class, I don't know why you are here. I think you are in the wrong school. You should be in Yale or Princeton."

"I applied to Berkeley."

"That's really bad, because it is a very liberal school." He sounded upset.

"I might go to Wellesley."

"That's even *worse*, because it's more liberal than Berkeley. That's where Hillary went!"

"..."

I couldn't understand why he believed that liberalism was so bad[53], and thought it was just simply a left/right power struggle.

Even though I received an 'A' grade in The Principals of Macroeconomics in 2009, I was still a proud defender of communism, although my professor was a staunch conservative[54]. With such a closed mind, it was so hard to digest opposing opinions. I would rather maintain my bias that my opponents were wrong or ignorant, instead of listening and then engaging in introspection.

---

[53] Now I understand that liberal ideology has positive aspects, but should only be applied in certain situations, mostly, in short term. Just like medicine, we only need them when the economy is seriously ill. Otherwise, conservative economic principles should govern, in accordance with human nature.

[54] Then, I still had no idea how ignorant I was, and could not realize that China's great economic achievement was the result of adopting the conservative economic principles of small government and greater individual freedom. Yes, this was what happened in 'Red China.'

So, the Bear kept warning me, "Hold your tongue and listen, keep an open mind…"

However, I thought I *was* listening and *had* an open mind, although I did not really understand that the word 'listening' involves a complicated process of thinking and research.

That spring, I graduated with Summa Cum Laude from Western Nevada College. I received an Academic Excellence Award in peer mentoring, and was invited to join Phi Theta Kappa, the honor society. When I thanked the president Dr. Carol Lucy for providing such highquality education, I told her that I was admitted to Wellesley College.

Dr. Lucy could not believe her ears and asked me twice, "Wesleyan?"

"No, Wellesley."

Dr. Lucy was so glad that she had a student admitted to Wellesley,

"You are the *trail blazer* of our school, because you are the first student admitted to Wellesley College. The school is lucky to have you, and I am so proud of you. You are a role model of our school."

I was so touched, because I thought my contribution for the school was minimal.

EMBRACED BY MY WELLESLEY SISTERS

In September 2009, the Bear accompanied me to the campus of the beautiful, famous, Wellesley College. It was exciting for both of us. I especially enjoyed my first convocation. It was inspiring as it was fun. The speakers were super intelligent and humorous. They encouraged us to be open-minded, to try to fully explore our potential, but take the time to develop sisterhood[55].

President Kim Bottomly was a wise, charming lady, successful both in science and management. In her welcome speech, she told us a story about how she decided to accept the President of Wellesley College. Before she was considered for this role, she was a scientist in Chemistry and a Dean at Yale University.

When she received the offer, she called several of her friends who were successful scientists. She learned that they had either received degrees from Wellesley College or married someone who received a degree from Wellesley College. So, she humorously concluded that, if one wants to be a successful scientist, she or he may either get education from Wellesley College, or marry one who was educated by Wellesley College.

She also eased some students' concern about difficulties in finding boyfriends since Wellesley has none on campus. She said:
"Wellesley has the reputation of making perfect women. You don't need to worry about no boy here, the Harvard men will come here to find you!" Right after she finished the sentence, many of the incoming freshmen got excited,
"Great, he will come here to find me!"

I truly enjoyed their excitement, because such topics had never been openly discussed during my life in China. President Bottomly also advised us not to study *too* hard and be sure to participate social activities. I also enjoyed the

---

[55] Each new student was assigned a peer mentor.

excitement when the provost and dean of the college, Andrew Shennan, told us,

"You are not the ordinary women, you are the women who will…"

"change the world!" the girls jumped and cheered.

After the convocation, I experienced my first Step Singing, which has been a tradition of Wellesley College for over a hundred years.

I so remember the beautiful Flower's Day ceremony at Houghton Chapel where President Kim Bottomly and other faculty members handed out flowers to welcome new sisters. I felt being embraced by this new environment, and no longer missed home. The Bear was happy for me, although he was sad to seperate from me.

Before the Bear left the school, he saved an ancient terrapin (and a college mascot) from a family who captured it from the school's Wanban Lake and was trying to bring it home for supper. That terrapin was *huge*; we saw it from far away when we were walking around the lake. The Bear saw a black woman jumping on the back of the terrapin, which was trying to escape, or bite her, or both.

He said to me:

"This creature has been in this lake probably for over one hundred years, they are going to boil it in oil, not fair! This antique should belong to the school." So, he took out his cell phone and called the campus police. In a couple of minutes, a cop car came and rescued the poor terrapin. Later, when the Bear told Susan, my dean, about this incident, Susan said, "that terrapin might be 280 years old." After he went back to Nevada, the Bear called me every day and asked me to bring food to feed the terrapin, or just simply say 'hello'.

INSPIRED BY MY WELLELEY SISTERS

I chose Classical Economics as my major and had to take an Econ-writing class. Professor Ann Velenchick gave us a quiz in the first class and most of us did not pass. We were so scared and read everything before her class. On the Friday of the second week, Ann told us that we would have no homework for that weekend, because she knew she provoked insomnia for two weeks and wanted us to relax. So, at dinner, I asked another Davis Scholar Estelle what she would do on Saturday. She told me that she was going to pick up trash as a volunteer, I told her that I would like to join her.

The next morning, Estelle drove me and two other students to Franklin Park in Boston. The park was so beautiful in the fall weather. We joined two dozen Wellesley Alumnae, and started to pull weeds.

I had not done manual labor for a long time, so I was very serious and worked hard. Before we returned the tools, I had blisters on both of my hands, but I truly enjoyed the day. When we were having our lunch of pizza, the Chairwoman of the Boston Wellesley Alumnae Association asked us whether we liked this activity and invited us to leave our emails on a form, so we could be invited to such activities in the future. All of us left our emails, but none of us could imagine the exciting invitation which would soon arrive!

MEETING WITH MADELINE ALBRIGHT

The following week, I received an email telling me that I was invited to meet the former secretary of state,

Madeline Albright. I thought it was a junk mail, so, I did not contact the person that I was asked to contact. At dinner, Estelle saw me and told me that all four of us who pulled the weeds at Franklin Park were invited to meet with the former Secretary of State Madeline Albright. I could not believe and asked her why. She told me that the Chairwoman of the Boston Wellesley Alumnae Association arranged this for us. We were so excited for this event to happen.

During the 1998 Asian Financial Crisis, I was fascinated by Madam Madeline Albright's work while she was the Secretary of the State. Although I was still politically immature, my Mom was always absorbed by stories of strong women who made differences to the world. She told me stories of Madam Sun Yat Shien, Madam Jiang Kai Shek and Mrs. Clinton. I remember my Mom mentioned about Madam Albright and commented on her strong will during the Kosovo War which my Mom watched on the news.

While my Mom was watching the news at my Shenzhen home, she saw the then most powerful woman in American history stand in front of a war airplane and explain the meaning of the Kosovo War to a German crowd. The news reporter said that Secretary Albright, who had to fled Hitler's regime as a child believed that the Kosovo War was also a morally defining mission for the U.S., and it would not permit ethnic cleansing.
Mom exclaimed,
"This woman is not simple; she is stronger than many strong men in the world."

Later, Mom kept following news about Secretary Albright and showed me her collection of clippings, stories and pictures of her. Mom also believed that Secretary Albright was a woman with extraordinary wisdom and charm. She loved talking about what Secretary Albright said, and how she dressed. So, when I got the chance to meet her in person, I knew this could excite my Mom and called her in the evening. Mom was so glad for me and wanted me to report to her after the meeting.

We went to the meeting and each of us received a beautiful book, *Read My Pins*, written by Madeline Albright, as a gift from the sponsor. After she gave a speech, we had a Q and A session. Some questions are quite inspiring. One guy asked her how the United States should deal with China's ripping off resources in Africa. She said that the U.S. should try to find mutual interests and work toward our common goals instead of focusing on differences between the two countries.

Meeting with Madeline Albright, Sep 2009

I was satisfied with this answer, and when I asked her to sign her book for me, she pleasantly did. In fact, I was too shy to say a word, and just smiled at her.

So, she greeted me,

"Hi, how are you today?"

"I am very well. Thank you so much for doing this for us. Could you please sign your book for me?"

"Sure, which year is your graduation year?"

"2011."

"Great! Here you go. Good luck to your studies at Wellesley."

CONTROVERSIAL CLASS DISCUSSIONS

Wellesley College had a grade deflation policy which meant that, no matter how wonderful your essay might be, if it doesn't express a unique point of view, it cannot be an 'A' essay. This implies that students might have to adopt extrem minority positions, and substantiate them with ample evidence to get an 'A'. Since I had gotten used to getting straight 'A's at my junior college, I thought I should aim for 'A's at Wellesley as well.

So, when professor Ann Vellenchik assigned us an Econ paper to evaluate Obama's Stimulus Packeage, I chose to criticize Obama's position, although I had knocked door to door to help elect him. Of course, my position was contrary to the opinion of the rest of the class and professor Vellenchik. I disputed the way Obama planned to spend the money, because his plan was mainly based on demand side economics.

I believed that the stimulus package should be mostly spent on supply side[56], because increased profit leads to expansion and create jobs, increased demand for imported goods could further impair the competitiveness of our industries. Besides, real entrepreneurs, who know how to grow businesses, know better how to efficiently use resources than the government. Government shouldn't risk tax payers' money to pick winners and losers. When government plays the role of God, it kills those really good entrepreneurs and let the wrong ones to stay in market, on the costs of the whole society's suffers.

When professor Vellenchick looked at my paper, she told me that I had to change my position, otherwise she could not give me a passing grade. I wouldn't give up, so, I wrote her a long email explaining my reasoning in more depth. The good thing is that professor Vellenchick is an honest scholar. After I listed my evidence and reasoning, she didn't counter my arguments. She gave me a B+ on the same paper that she would have given an F.

Professor Vellenchick and I also had a dispute concerning minimum wage. She believed that minimum wage could help the poor, I believed minimum wage may cause higher unemployment rate and higher prices of goods, both hurt the poor. My reasoning was that, since the prices of goods equal to marginal costs, higher wages result in higher prices of goods. So, instead of spending $20/hour to hire one

---

[56] There was very weak voice of the supply side economics at Wellesley College. So, most of the students just took whatever their professors told them as truth. I found this problematic, because it made a half of the country believe that Reaganomics doesn't work whick is untrue.

worker and this worker could buy one steak (produced by another person) with that $20, we could spend that $20 dollars to hire ten workers at $2/hour and these ten workers could buy ten steaks for $2 each. This means that we could feed 20 people with that $20-dollar transaction, instead of feeding two people only. Besides, increased price of goods could impair our industries competitiveness in the international market, further hurt the poor. Professor Vellenchick agreed with my reasoning but still insisted on a minimum wage increase when the economy recovered.

Then, the final paper she assigned us was to identify one major cause that triggered this Great Recession, in three double-spaced pages. This was a challenging task, because we had read thousands of pages concerning this topic. I thought it impossible to summarize the whole picture in three pages. So, I asked professor Vellenchik whether we were allowed to write the paper in an entertaining way. She replied, "That will be a plus!"

So, I made up a 'tarnished woman' story to describe what happened. Here it is:

IF ONLY WE HAD NOT CHANGED THE MONETARY POLICY SO RADICALLY...

Not long ago, there were two women and a gentleman. One was a lady from the royal family and the other one was a beautiful slut with sexually transmitted diseases (STD). The gentleman was from a rich family holding close to seventy trillion dollars in cash, and he faced the choice of marrying one of the two women.

It was the tradition in his family that men only married ladies from royal or noble families, and would not give a slut a second glance. But, this time, this gentleman's family was totally confused, because not only did this royal lady present as a total bore, but her father announced in this case he would reduce the dowry of his daughter to less than 20% of what he provided in the past for his other daughters. At the same time, the father of the charming looking slut, who was introduced as a triple 'A' rated lady by a matchmaker, announced that he would provide a handsome dowry for whoever marries his daughter.

The family of the gentleman eventually decided to allow their son to marry the slut, not knowing of her provenance. The result of this marriage was, of course, two unhappy losers. The slut passed her diseases to the gentleman, and her father could not deliver the dowry he promised.

The gentleman was ruined because he could not determine the nature of his disease, and how serious it was. He felt as though the end of the world was at hand. He wondered how the hell this slut could be disguised as a triple A rated lady by recognized world class experts, and what might have been the outcome if the other royal lady hadnot been so boring, and her dad hadnot reduced her dowry so significantly.

In reality, the name of the royal lady is 'Federal Funds' and her father's name is Alan Greenspan. The name of the slut is 'Subprime Collateral Debt Obligation' (S-CDO) and her father's name is Wall Street Investment Bankers. The rich gentleman represents a $70 trillion dollars global pool of savings that has to be safely and conservatively invested. But there are more than two losers in this story. The result of marrying the global pool of money to the S-CDOs is this unprecedented international financial crisis that we are experiencing today.

This financial crisis could have been averted if the Federal Open Market Committee, controlled by Alan Greenspan, had not made 13 cuts in the federal funds rate, lowering it from 6.5% in May 2000 to 1% in June 2003. Greenspan announced to the public that this monetary policy would hold steady for a while (Bert Ely 2009)[57]. This decision made federal bonds absurdly unattractive and pushed the global pool of money into the mortgage backed security market, which managers thought as safe as federal bonds.

Seventy trillion dollars is a powerful enough incentive to both make people lie and become irrationally creative. When there was not enough credit worthy mortgage backed securities to absorb the giant pool of money, Wall Street

---

[57] Ely, Bert, (2009), Bad Rules Produce Bad Outcomes: Underlying Public-Policy Causes of the U.S. Financial Crisis, The CATO Journal, An Interdisciplinary Journal of Public Policy Analysis, Volume 29 Number 1, Winter 2009. Retrieved from:

http://www.cato.org/pubs/journal/cj29n1/cj29n1.html

bankers intentionally lowered their credit standards and let anyone who wanted to buy a house obtain a loan.

This manully increased demand further pushed housing prices to record highs. The Wall Street bankers knew that nothing can go up forever except people's ages. They knew those loans were risky and toxic but thought if they mixed triple C rated subprime mortgage loans with triple A or double A rated mortgage loans, then the possibility of loan defaults could be controlled within a reasonable range. So, they employed computer software to slice millions of mortgages into billions of shares, renamed them CDOs, and sold them to the giant pool of money as triple A securities. Most of them were so rated by Standard & Poor's.

If the giant pool of money had never been spent to buy subprime CDOs, people might never have had the chance to enter into subprime mortgages to buy houses that they could not afford. The housing bubble might never have occurred at the first place. This money should have placed in diverse investments, particularly to fund industries that were booming.

When everyone who wanted a house had already bought one with money borrowed from banks through mortgage brokers with credit based on no clarification of income, assets and pulse, the prices of houses stopped rising. The housing bubbles popped. The borrowers of the subprime mortgages could no longer borrow additional money from banks to pay for their mortgages. Some of them never made a single payment before the housing bubbles burst. The chain of mortgage backed securities broke, and CDOs became worthless.

Every individual and financial entity ensnared by this chain began to choke. The subprime mortgage borrowers have lost their life savings, condemned to live with unresolved debt for the rest of their life. The mortgage brokers who ran their businesses on borrowed money had to file bankruptcy, and the big banks had to accept federal bailout funds to survive. The whole financial system became deadly ill. No wonder, when people spend $70 trillion dollars to buy any one type of goods, pricing bubbles of those goods will be sure to result.

A marriage based on lies cannot last long; neither can an economy based on false credit. The gentleman in our story eventually reversed his life by divorcing the slut and marrying the royal lady, despite her small dowry. He finally realized that health, and asset safety, are the most important elements for a normal family life. The managers of the giant pool of money realized that their only safe harbor is federal bonds and now they stick with them no matter how low the interest rate is. But the catastrophic loss of the giant pool of money might never be remedied.

When I presented my paper to professor Vellenchik, she saw the word "slut" and said,
"What? Is it true that you have the word "slut" in an Econ paper?" I noded.

She grabed the paper and swiftly read it.

"Jin Lan, I knew you were smart, but I didn't know you were this smart!" I was glad that she loved this paper.

At the beginning of the last class of the semester, professor Vellenchik made a delicious lunch for us. After we took our food and drinks to our seats, professor Vellenchik announced that she was going to read a paper to the class without permission from the writer. So, she read my paper with a big grin.

After she finished, the whole class was excited and asked who wrote this paper.

A student said,

"It must be Jin Lan!" I smiled.

Another student said,

"Jin Lan, you made us don't know how to write!" I was so glad for the acceptance of my writing with my broken English. When I couldn't speak English fluently like the rest of the class, I always felt stupid.

Professor Vellenchik gave me an A- for this Econ writing course and said that this class was exceptionally smart, sounded like she didn't plan to give me an A. No wonder, because her 13 students were from 13 countries. We were all rare animals in our own nations.

***

Another controversial discussion was about International Trade. The mainstream economists, like my professor LeBrune, believed that WTO shouldn't impose terms to protect fair trade, because they believe all trade deals create win-win results. Their excuse is that, in the long run, when emerging economies are fully developed, the wages of the loser countries will start to increase.

However, shouldn't they remember Keynes' warning, "in the long run, we are all dead"? In the long run, our rivals, who do not share our values, will enslave all of us. The inevitable consequence of avoiding shortterm pain is longterm pain.

When professor LeBrune raised the question whether WTO should impose rules to protect human rights and the environment, I was the only one believed it should, but she dismissed that idea without allowing further discussion. It is similar as Big Bang theory is not allowed to be doubted, because the majority of the scientists agree with each other. Well, the majority of the people on earth believed that the Sun circled the earth before the opposite was proven.

Professor LeBrune was a sweetheart, but her refusal to debate mainstream economic theories limited the depth of class discussion. Such a teaching style could produce close-minded students at very young age. This is one of the major reasons this book is dedicated to all kindhearted *progressive* people and *young* people on earth.

Through further education, I discovered that fairness or unfairness can be exported or imported through trade by trade treaties. Win-win results only exist in those markets where effective rule of law guarantee fair competitions. When a free worker competes in the same market with slaves, such worker is essentially treated as the equal of the slaves.

I believe if WTO won't impose terms to protect Fair and Free trade to improve justice, the developed countries should impose terms of basic human rights and environment protections in bilateral trade treaties, because they have purchasing and investment power. Such power may disappear when emerging economies mature.

***

Herewith another story about mainstream beliefs. I took two Feminist Economics classes from our only Marxist professor, Julie Matthaei. I learned a lot from her, but I did not agree with everything she said. For example, she believed that Marxism died and didn't apply to the modern world. I pointed out that Marxism not only didn't die, it had already succeeded in the West while capitalism was succeeding in China. I provided my evidence such as, the welfare system, the Anti-Trust law, Affirmative Action laws, Worker's Union protections and the like, to prove that Marxism had influenced the West significantly and was still alive. On the other side, the two-digital growth for decades in deregulated China, proved the efficiency of capitalism.

Then professor Matthaei had to agree with me and said that I had advantages over the rest of the class, because of my life experience in China allowed me to identify communist/capitalist features easily. However, I had no idea about my inability to identify social injustice, because I lived my entire life in a system without it, and got used to it. When professor Matthaei asked me,
"You don't believe there is repression in China, do you?"
My first reaction in my mind was,
"Of course I don't, you think China is a branch of hell?"

However, after thought about a few moments, I realized that repression has always been in front of my eyes. I just never could recognize it. For example, the "Hu Kou" system restricted people's freedom of migration and movement. It confined generations of peasants to the agricultural land and limited educational opportunities for their children.

This system might not be intended to repress the peasants, but that was the effect. It partially answers though, why China developed much faster than most other countries after its consistent deregulation. Over regulation is also one of the major reasons why the American Empire fell, although the majority of the Americans are blind to this fact.

Professor Matthaei was the third person who saw through my seriously brainwashed mind and pointed out. The first one was my cousin's wife Olivia who was a beautiful cardiologist in Los Altos, CA. She told me I was brainwashed, within 15 minutes after I walked into her house. The second one was my mother in law Doris. She was the one who tactically questioned me,
"Who are *we*?" Because when answering her, I would respond:
"We think…" instead of "I think…" for questions about my independent opinions. I didnot know that a person couldn't be free if he or she couldn't have independent opinions. I did not appreciate their criticisms when they pointed out the truth, because the truth hurts.

Later, I realized that most Chinese people, including me, had very little understanding about the word "democracy." In the summer of 2010, I went to China and had no access to Facebook. So, I could not get in touch with my Wellesley sister, Ashley H. Harmon, a successful ballerina.

I could see from my email that people were talking to me on Facebook, but I could not respond to them. I felt so sorry but thought it was normal that I was not allowed to use

Facebook in China, because we always lived this way. After I returned to school and bumped into Ashley on campus, I apologized to her for being out of touch due to no access to Facebook.

She so empathetically gave me a big hug, "I am so sorry for you, Jin Lan, we Americans are so spoiled and take democracy for granted."

Her reaction not only surprised me, but also called up my memory of Li Ping, a retired CCTV[58] hostess, who proudly bragged that she had never voted "No" in the People's Congress[59]. Both Ashley Harmon, American ballerina, and Li Ping, a CCTV celebrity, were artists. However, by contrast, Li Ping was politically immature, especially, as a deligate of the People's Congress. She clearly didn't know what democracy meant.

As for me, I had never connected the Great Firewall to democracy before. I thought that all of our rights were bestowed by the communist party. Chinese society had no concept of 'natural rights.'

AN EPIPHANEY ABOUT
THE UNIVERSE/ GOD/THE CREATOR

The students at Wellesley were much more open minded than in my former school, so I could challenge religious views that I did not dare before. When I heard a student, who was a Christian, question,

---

[58] China Central TV station.
[59] Some Chinese celebrities can directly be the representatives of people in People's congress or political bureau.

"If human beings evolved from monkeys, why are the monkeys still there and did not become human beings?"
As an atheist, without thinking for a second,
"I can answer that question."
"Go ahead."
"You know, not all the girls can study in Wellesley College, so, not all monkeys could become human beings."
The class broke into laughter.
"Did I say anything wrong?"
"No, no, no, you are right," the girls responded.

At this time, I was still an atheist. I thought that creationism and evolution doctrines were mutually exclusive, because my girlfriend Colleen, who was a Christian, didn't believe in evolution. After I studied more physics, chemistry, biology, the Bibles, Taoism and Buddhism and the like, I realized that creationism and evolution could coexist perfectly.

If, according to Buddhism, everything exists for a reason, then what is the origin of everything? The origin must be the energy source of the universe, and it governs/communicates with everything in the universe by the rule of the nature, from the micro to the macro. I call the energy source of the universe God/the Creator, because it has a perpetual life, it created everything in the universe, and no one can challenge the all mighty rule of nature. It is likely there are an infinite number of universes in the Space. They can merge or split, but they can never cancel each other out, because energy has constant life. They can change their forms of existence but will never disappear.

So, here is my vision of the unity of the Universe/God/the Creator. It is formed by a Large White Hole and a Large Black Hole. The Large White Hole has an infinite number of smaller white holes and black holes, but none of them have constant life, because all of them will end up in the Large Black Hole.

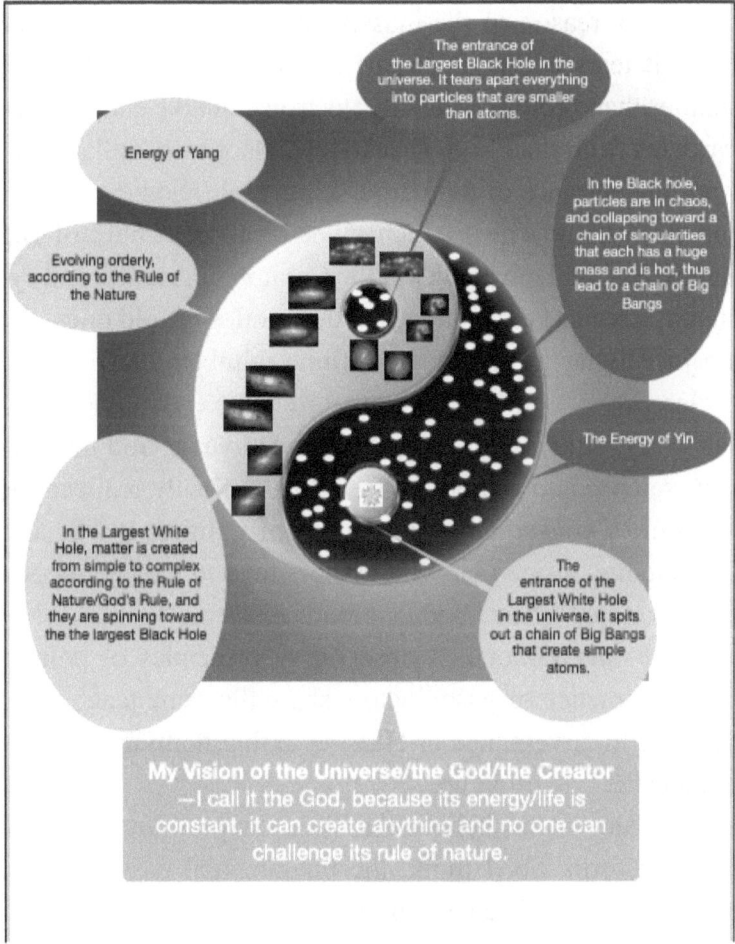

At the entrance of the Large White Hole, a chain of Big Bangs spit out elementary particles. With time, these particles form subatomic particles and atoms, molecues and the like. Then these matters evolve from simple to complex according to the unchallengeable Rule of Nature, with everything spinning towards the entrance of the Large Black Hole due to gravity.

By reason of the massive mass of the Large Black Hole, it tears everything apart into basic particles that are smaller than protons, such as, electrons, quarks and leptons. Particles from the Large Black Hole chaotically collapse toward the entrance of the Large White Hole (Some scientists call this 'singularity') which gives birth to a chain of Big Bangs. So, the Universe/God/the Creator/ constantly and cyclically creates new matters and dismantles the old ones. We are just living in one of the infinite numbers of Big Bang cycles.

By studying the nature of the Universe/God/the Creator, science and ancient philosophies, I finally realized the wisdom of conservative priniciples of politics. It was also enlightening to me that wise doctors tend to let Mother Nature take care of our bodies before resorting to medical or surgical interventions. Conservative principles of politics and the practice of wise doctors share the same teaching of Taoism: In governance or Healing, doing nothing that contradicts the rule of nature.

Taoists also believe that the most profound takes the simplest form. So, I think, the fundamental rule of nature must be gravity. We can observe this truth from the movements of galaxies, clouds, atoms, animals and human behavior. In order to last, all such entities must guard their energy. This implies that self love is necessary to be able to give away true love. So the balance between give and take is maintained, and the environment is healthy and peaceful. Self love is different than selfishness which only takes energy and never returns it.

POLITICALLY AWAKENING

I really enjoyed everything and everyone in school. Especially, my classmates who determined to change the world. A Davis Scholar, Estelle, told me that 50% of the Wellesley women want to change the world, and the rest of the 50% want to take it over. Such ambitions sound so normal in America, but it can be problematic in many other societies.

One night, it was almost 2:00 am, our dorminitory fire alarm rang. The fire trucks came, and we all ran out with very few clothes on. While the fire fighters were searching our rooms, the red and blue lights on the firetrucks were flashing. With our funny clothes and the flashing lights, we felt like having a party.

So, I grabbed a cell phone from a Davis Scholar, Jezi and started to take video of everyone. No one tried to avoid me except a black girl, who ran away from me, so I chased her to record her for fun. She said, "No, no, no!" to me, but I did not stop. When the fire fighters left, I returned the cell phone to Jezi and went back to sleep.

At this point, it was almost 3:00 am.

Someone knocked at my door. It was that black girl who tried to avoid the camera.

She asked me to have Jezi delete the video, because it might negatively affect her when, in the future, she runs for president in her country. I did not know, then, that fire alarm was set off by her hair spray. So, I didn't take it seriously, and refused to do so.

The next day, she wrote me a long email. I realized that she was serious and asked Jezi to delete the video. Jezi agreed and deleted it.

In 2015, when I was talking about cultural gaps with a very successful high school classmate, Lisa, at her home in China, I told this story. Lisa's reaction was beyond my expectation. I thought she got used to the reality of Chinese politics like me, but it made her upset that, as a citizen of a socalled 5,000 years old civilization, she could not share the same dream that the African girl had.

The debate about whether China should adopt western democracy has been going on for a long time. I have switched my position back and forth several times. I still have not reached a conclusion, because I saw how a free society, such as the United States, can also be brainwashed with one idea or the other. This can occur by peer pressure or the abandonment of independent thinking. Democracy doesn't really set us free, but the understanding of God/Nature can.

Although still an authoritarian political system, by 2016, China had already achieved enviable economic success. Its GDP reached $11.19 trillion dollars, from $195.9 billion in 1981, a 55X increase in 35 years. For the same time period, the US GDP grew at less than five times. So, China's achievement is quite amazing. Of course, its military muscles are also strengthened accordingly.

Now, 90% of Chinese housings are private. Of those homes, 80% of them are owned outright, without mortgages or any other leans, according to Forbes[60]. It also built an amazing world class infrastructure from almost nothing. China has been exporting and financing infrastructure development capacity worldwide. 35,000kms of highspeed railway and 60 modern airports have been constructed in the last 11years. Chinese tourists no longer were satisfied with only domestic travel. Their footprints are now everywhere. By 2019, 26+ million Chinese visited the US, while fewer than one million Americans visited China. Yet, China's national debt only increased by $3.7 trillion dollars during 2008-2016.

As a Chinese immigrant, I am very proud of the achievement of my motherland. Yet I didn't really understand that the foundation of these achievements should be largely credited to Reaganomics[61] and China's right wing leaning authoritarian regime which embraced ancient Chinese wisdom of Tao[62]. Imagine the result if, every five or ten years, China reverted to playing Owellian government games like the Cultural Revolution. Its position in the world today could be quite different.

I don't mean that China should stay an authoritarian regime forever. I just realized that every society should evolve on their own pace with a bit of push from outside. Rushing to overdo anything may be destructive to other parts of the world. An example is the Mideast. Any good medicine can be misused by an overdose.

---

[60] https://www.forbes.com/sites/wadeshepard/2016/03/30/how-people-in-china-afford-their-outrageously-expensive-homes/#23ab4cf4a3ce
[61] Reaganomics = Trickledown Economics = Supplyside Economics.
[62] Lao Tzu believed that, when the master governs, the people hardly aware that he exists.

THE FALLING AMERICAN EMPIRE

When the last Great Recession hit America in 2008, I thought the economy could be healed by the time I graduated from Wellesely College in 2012, because I saw how China rapidly recovered and thrived from the Asian Financial Crisis. We Chinese people see a crisis as an opportunity of rebirth/rejuvenation. So, I didn't take this Great Recession seriously, and expected the Obama administration to revive the economy sooner than Reagan did, because we had repeatedly heard the liberal mantra that "It is proved that Trickle-down Economics doesn't work". It took Reagan, who implemented Trickle-down economic policies, to create 16 million jobs in eight years, I thought, Obama's smarter strategy would create more jobs within a shorter time.

However, my optimism didn't get me very far. Obama's eight years increased 36 percentage points of National Debt to GDP ratio[63], but only achieved 27% of GDP growth[64] and 12 million new jobs. When one compares to Reagan's 63% of GDP growth and 16 million new jobs achieved by increasing 18 percentage points of National Debt to GDP ratio, one can be truly disappointed with the incessant preaching of demand side economics in western countries.

For the past eight years, not only myself but many of my Wellesley alumnae had to endure hopes betrayed and

---

[63] https://www.macrotrends.net/1381/debt-to-gdp-ratio-historical-chart

[64] https://www.thebalance.com/us-gdp-by-year-3305543

shattered, again, again and again. Although I have a family which provide me a roof and food, watching bridges and overpasses become roofs for the hundreds of thousands of homeless people in California[65], encountering a beautiful elegantly dressed lady begging me for a few dollars to buy food in a supermarket, healthy middle aged men holding signs that say "work for food" on the roadside in the icy cold winter, frequently reading desperate posts from my Wellesley Alumnae on Facebook, many of them were unemployed or underemployed with multiple jobs but still living under poverty lines, my employer had to close its 30+ year old business that was the industry leader in the world…my heart broke, and I asked everyday with great sorrows, '**What went wrong, America? Isn't this the *Land of the Free*? If people can't grow, how can we be free?**'

    I couldn't find an answer from the liberal dominated mainstream media. It didn't even believe the American Empire was falling. When Mr. Trump was running for president with his promise of "Make America Great Again", President Obama fought back, stating that "America is already great, with no need to be greater." Even though I remained frozen in the situation, seeing no growth opportunity, I never doubted the theory of American Exceptionalism. Until, that is Mr. Trump won the 2016 presidential election and our beloved alumna Madam Hillary R. Clinton lost. Why? Because, the Nobel laureate economist Paul Krugman predicted that the stockmarket would go down if Mr. Trump won, but the result turned out to be the opposite.

---

[65] https://www.foxnews.com/us/homelessness-los-angeles-california-crisis-death-rate-report

So, I thought, if professor Krugman's prediction was wrong, then, the economic theories I had previously believed must be flawed. To find out the truth, I withheld my lifelong liberal biases, and intentionally listened to the conservative critics that I previously thought to be motivated by selfishness and greed. Then I did my research and present you my journey of discovery.

WHO IS TO BLAME?

The best-selling author and filmmaker, Peter Navarro, who wrote *Death By China,* believes that the fall of the American Empire is caused by China. I found that perception to be as shortsighted as Chairman Mao's blaming China's Great Famine on the Soviet Union. So, who was the one sharp enough to point out, in depth, the true causations of the fall? Mr. Trump! He demonstrated that it was excessive spending on policing the world, bad trade policies and unfriendly business policies brought down America. I could't understand him then, but I understand him now.

During his 2016 presidential campaign, Mr. Trump repeatedly mentioned that America should take care of ourselves first, and not police the world. Although I couldn't agree with him since Wellesley women are expected to change the world, what he said echoed the Economics 101 textbook. People who took this course should know the typical 'opportunity cost' graph that depicts how resources are scarce, if they are used to produce more guns, less butter will flow into the market.

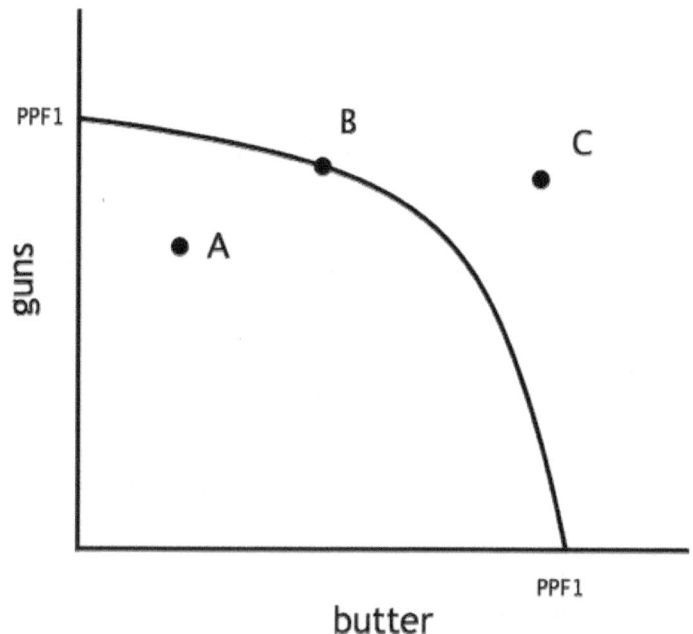

The histories of the Roman Empire and the Soviet Union again validated this rule. They both collapsed. If China hadnot changed its policy direction in the 1980's, it could have collapsed, too. China learned this theory from top American economists and consistently implemented their development reforms for decades with the guidance of Reaganomics. However, America forgot the lesson it lectured the world, because certain political elites made most of the Americans believe in the theory of American Exceptionalism.

Whenever I mentioned Taoism or Buddhism in a debate with my Wellesley alumnae, they always counter with the phrase, "America is different" which means ancient wisdom from any society doesn't apply to it. Well, human history has proved that, while many societal differences exist, all share a common trait, that is, mistakes are repeated over and over again, horizontally and vertically. And, if we keep doing the same thing, we shouldn't expect to create a different outcome.

In his campaign speeches, Mr. Trump also repeatedly mentioned that our trading partners, like China and Mexico, had taken advantages of the United States through unfair free trade for decades. However, he blamed the real fault to America's bad policies that punished our own businesses and diminished entrepreneurial spirit for decades, instead our trading partners. I couldn't believe him, because I was still biased against him and almost all conservative/pro-capitalist policies, due to my stubborn liberal ideology. So, I wrote a Facebook post on the 2016 Thanksgiving night as follows:

Jin Lan Deng
November 25, 2016

I am glad that we had a civilized Thanksgiving dinner and discussion about Trump without any damage. One of our Trump supporters pointed out that, in the Bible, Nehemiah rebuilt the walls to protect Jerusalem and all Trump's kids married Jewish people, maybe Trump was sent by God to make America Great Again. I asked my husband, after the walls rebuilt, what happened to the Jews? He said that they were thrown out and spread to all over the world. Then, I said, we have a famous Great Wall, before we built this wall, we had Confucius, Taoist, Suntz...such great thinkers like Socrates and Shakya Mani. After the Great Wall was built, we no longer be able to think. That is why China has been repeating history for thousands of years, still hard to improve. Today, Jewish people are so successful in the countries without walls. So, I believe, walls can not make people stronger but more ignorant and less competitive. I wish Trump will be inspired by someone who is smart and around him, so he can understand and won't withdraw TPP, the smartest treaty in human history and truly can make America great forever.

Linda Kosinski, Alyssa Jennifer Baringer and 3 others   16 Comments

I thought this argument was brilliant. What I couldn't understand was the difference between a temporary solution and a longterm solution. Temporary solutions are prefatory for long term solutions. Mr. Trump's Wall ideas were just temporary solutions to begin to solve the immediate crisis of immigration and trade inbalance. Sadly, more than a half of the country can't understand him, and believe he is undereducated and ignorant.

I also didn't realize that free trade could benefit both trading partners only when the both parties enjoy the same effective rule of law. Otherwise, free workers can be enslaved when they are put in the same market to compete with slaves. It's not even the American corporations' fault, they have to cut the costs to survive.

Mr. Trump identified three major causes that brought down America, he forgot that the Federal Reserve Board was at fault too. My Wellesley professor Daniel Sichel, who was a senior associate director at the Fed under Ben Bernanke, told us that the Fed has two major goals to guide their monetary polices. The first goal is full employment, the second goal is 2% inflation. This means when the unemployment rate is above 5%, the Fed will implement expansionary monetary policies; when the inflation rate exceeded 2%, the Fed will implement contractionary monetary policies. These ideas sounded reasonable for me when I was in school, but now I find them problematic.

First, the 5% unemployment rate benchmark, considered as full employment rate, can't reflect the true picture of the economy, especially after long recessions that discouraged numerous people to give up seeking jobs. For example, the labor force participation in 2000 was above 67%, yet in

2019, it's only a bit more than 63%[66]. Since this last recession depleted the resources of a lot of families, we can't optimistically believe that over ten million people just went home and are enjoying retirement. How many of them can afford that luxury, with such out of control healthcare costs, the burdern of high interest student loans, and heavy mortgages?

Second, the 2% inflation target doesn't accurately depict the true status of the economy since it can be deflated by globalization. For example, the famous exchange equation provides:

$$GDP = PY = MV$$

Which means that if the quantity of real output (Y) and the speed of money circulation (V) hold constant, then, the increase of money supply (M) shoud affect price level (P) with the same multiplyer.

However, the Fed had expanded its balancesheet almost 4 folds[67] between 2008 and 2016, but the inflation rates stayed less than 1.65% for six out of the eight years[68].

Professor Sichel believed that the Fed printed money was just sleeping on the banks' balancesheets, because it wasn't worth it for them to lend, since companies were not making profit even though the interest rate was close to 0%.

---

[66] https://www.thebalance.com/labor-force-participation-rate-formula-and-examples-3305805
[67] https://seekingalpha.com/article/4239837-really-worry-feds-balance-sheet
[68] https://inflationdata.com/Inflation/Inflation_Rate/HistoricalInflation.aspx

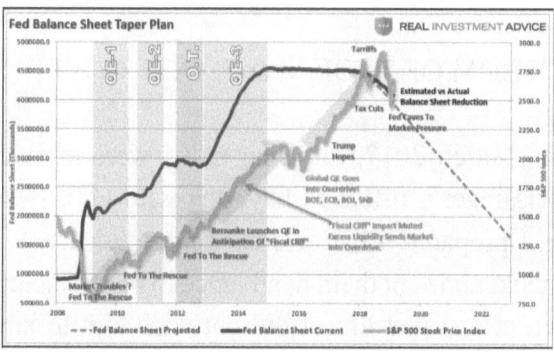

I had no argument for him then, but I found it wasn't true now. Let's look at China's foreign reserve record. It had less than $375 billion dollars of foreign debt in the end of 2008[69], but by 2019, its foreign debt reached almost $2 trillion dollars[70]. The biggest lender of the world obviously is the US since it has the largest economy of the world. The trillions of dollars of printed money, in fact, weren't sleeping on our banks' balancesheets, they went to where it has gravity (which in this context means smart and attractive policies.)

The Fed expanded its assets almost 4-fold under all Americans' credit, but about a half of the expanded assets went to fast-developing China. With the third highest corporate tax rate in the world (before Trump's tax cuts), America's big government policies made its growth almost impossible, even though the interest rates were kept so low for eight years. Businesses won't expand when there is no expected profit. If president Trump didn't cut the corporate tax rates by fourteen percentage points and killed 1000+ regulations, the situation could be much worse now.

---

[69] http://news.ifeng.com/mainland/200904/0424_17_1124424.shtml
[70] http://www.gov.cn/xinwen/2019-03/30/content_5378233.htm

THE WISDOM OF TAOISM & SMALL GOVERNMENT

In March 2017, the Bear and I were invited to Dr. Henry Kissinger's office to have tea with him. Before this meeting, I prepared a list of questions to ask Dr. Kissinger for my book, and sent them in advance to his assistant Sheila. However, after I met him, I did not wish him to labor over my questions, because I did not wish him to labor over my questions, and I could not use such a sweet, hard working 94-yearold gentleman for my benefit.

I only wanted him to have a break, because, when we were sitting in the waiting room, we saw him saying 'goodby' to a couple at the elevator, then welcome another couple to his office, and walked *them* to the elevator when the meeting was over. Then, he came to the waiting room to welcome us.

With Dr. Kissinger @ His Office in New York, 2018

A 94-yearold gentleman had such a tight schedule, and yet still insisted welcoming everyone and escorting them to the elevator. Such a noble spirit is so admirable and touching. So, when Dr. Kissinger asked about the letter that I sent to him, I told him I had only one question, that was,
"How are you?"

He said he was very well. He mentioned his beloved wife Nancy, who broke her hip during their trip in France, and his son David who was on the waiting list of the Bohemian Club. This surprised me, because people like him in China don't need to be on the waiting list of clubs. They would be fought for by the clubs.

Dr. Kissinger asked:
"How did you two meet each other?"
"*You* made us meet."
"What did I do?"
"You went to China to meet Mao, otherwise, the Bear and I could never meet each other."
"Sounds like I did the right thing."
"You did. You changed China and the world. Chinese people appreciate you. All of my Chinese friends want me to say 'hello' to you, and one of them gave you this very special tea." Dr. Kissinger humbly smiled and accepted the special oriental tea.

Dr. Kissinger also mentioned that he had been to my hometown Chongqing five times and expressed his admiration for Chinese people's family ethics. He complimented our appreciation of education and mutual support among family members. In the end, he insisted accompanying us to the elevator, no matter how hard we tried to stop him. So, I gave him a big hug at the elevator, and waved goodbye to him through tears.

Even by then, my mind was still very liberal and biased against conservative ideology, because I believed that all conservatives were selfish and greedy, that they were all about helping the rich to become richer and didn't care about the society. I wondered why people as wise and kind as Dr. Kissinger called themselves conservatives. Then, several events in the following years began to answer my question.

One was a visit, in the summer of 2017, to an 85-yearold sick man liveing alone in Lake Tahoe. This man had cancer. So, the Bear asked me to make some food to bring to his house every so often.

This man was a self-made conservative who made his wealth as a construction contractor. He could easily hire someone to take care of his errands, but he insisted to do everything himself even though he was so sick. When we finished eating, I wanted to clean up the dishes, he stopped me and said, "What is an American? It means, we take care of ourselves."

It was remarkable that he took pride in taking care of himself until the end of his life and refused to accept excessive assistance. Then he complained about the liberals who spoiled the world by 'over giving'. His charactor inspired me to question my bias, because he was about to die and had no reason to be selfish or greedy. He was saving every dollar to leave to his adopted children.

Another event was visiting the British Parliament in May 2018. At the House of Lords, the conservative whip, lord Borwick explained how the Houses of Parliament work:

"When something bad happens, the Labour Party tends to react aggressively and propose new laws to prevent the bad things from happening again. However, such laws usually have more negative side effects than good. So, my party's job is to try our best to delay the proposed laws to be further discussed or passed."

What Lord Borwick said echoed the recommendation of my conservative doctor when I had an injured knee, "Let Mother Nature takes care of it first."

My bias started to crumble, because it reminded me the wisdom of *Wu Wei Er Zhi,* by Lao Tzu, "When the master governs, people are hardly aware he exists."

2500 years ago, he wrote in his *The Book of the Virtue of the Way*: [71]

"If you want to be a great leader,
You must learn to follow the Tao[72],
Stop trying to control.
Let go of fixed plans and concepts,
And the world will govern itself.

The more prohibitons you have,
The less virtuous people will be.
The more weapons you have,
The less secure people will be.
The more subsidies you have,
The less self-reliant people will be.

---

[71] https://fee.org/articles/liberty-and-small-government-in-tao-te-ching/

[72] Tao means the way or path.

Therefore the Master says:
I let go of the law,
And people become honest.
I let go of economics,
And People become prosperous.
I let go of religion,
And people become serene.
I let go of all desire for the common good,
And the good becomes common as grass.

'Letting go'' is also one of the major wisdoms of Buddhism[73]. I realized that the wisdom of 'letting go' not only applies to the relationships between the government and the people, but also applies to the relationships between parents and children, love relationships, business relationships, and the like. Over-control and over-giving are both human behaviors pretending to be God when we can never be as wise and powerful as God. The results usually just backfire.

Everyday, I read hundreds of Facebook posts by my kindhearted and highly educated liberal sisters from the Seven Sisters College Alumnae. They repeat the same dogmas with which I was injected since birth, and they believe the far left is far better informed than the conservatives. They want the government to act as the God, so it can provide us education, healthcare, clean environment, defense, safety, justice…for free.

Dear readers, my life journey showed us how all of the 'free' things looked like under Mao, and how Trickle-

---

[73] https://www.huffpost.com/entry/the-art-of-mindfully-lett_b_5929270

down economics magically gave the barefeet Chinese abundant lives. So, I felt the urgency to remind the Americans to revalue the devalued conservative/ancient wisdom. Let everyone be himself/herself, and prosperity will naturally result. We don't need the government to give us anything for free. We can thrive only when the government leaves the businesses alone.

AFTERWORD

Dear readers,

Thank you very much for accompanying me on the bumpy rollercoaster ride over five decades. I hope you enjoyed this adventure and are inspired to create your own vision of the world. Life is unpredictable, but if we could help clear up some fallacies that can signaficantly affect our lives, the world will be a better place.

So, dear readers, if you agree with me, I hope you can help promote the devalued conservative wisdoms and spread my messages to the rest of the world:

1) *'It is proved that Trickle-down Economics doesn't work'* is a lie!

The famous Deng Xiao Ping quote: *'Let some people get rich first'* made China rocket from a backward country to the envy of the world and proved Trickle-down economics worked for 40 years. The deterioration of income polarization in the US was not caused by Trickle-down policies but their absence, because we had the third highest corporate tax rate in the world before Trump's tax cuts. Our high taxes diverted our resources to develop other countries instead of our own.

AFTERWORD

2) *'A Living wage helps the poor people'* is a lie!

It is a lie, because the prices of conventional market goods equal the marginal cost of the goods. When labor costs go up, the prices of goods increase accordingly. So, when the law requires a living wage that is higher than the market price of labor, people pay more for their living expenses while facing higher unemployment pressure.

Dear readers, if you don't agree with me, you are welcome to debate with me @jinlanmccann on Twitter. Your opinions will be greatly appreciated. Thank you!

This book would have been impossible without the generous and unconditional support from my husband William D. McCann, my Wellesley alumna Linda Kosinski, my dear friends Daniel C. Tiernan and James Ferreira. No words can express my gratitude to them. Their smallest gesture, and every word of comfort and encouragement will be remembered forever.

With School Flower @ Bashu High School, 1984

Cruise Ship Sailors on the Yangtze River, 1988

Bashu High School Classmates Welcoming the Bear, 2004

Bronze Letter Opener By Jin Lan @ Wellesley College, 2011

With Davis Scholars Lily & Dulo @ Wellesley College, 2011

With Davis Scholars Liza & Alyssa @ Wellesley College, 2011

With Davis Scholars @ Wellesley College, 2009

With President Kim Bottomly @ 2011 Commencement

Class Reunion with Ashley & Fiona, 2016

Class Reunion, 2016

With Davis Scholar Ashley H. Harmon, 2016

Genoa, Nevada, 2018

Chongqing, China, 2014

London, 2018

$19.99
ISBN 978-0-9989899-4-5

www.ingramcontent.com/pod-product-compliance
Lightning Source LLC
Chambersburg PA
CBHW020417010526
44118CB00010B/301